Program Authors

Peter Afflerbach

Camille Blachowicz

Candy Dawson Boyd

Wendy Cheyney

Connie Juel

Edward Kame'enui

Donald Leu

Jeanne Paratore

P. David Pearson

Sam Sebesta

Deborah Simmons

Sharon Vaughn

Susan Watts-Taffe

Karen Kring Wixson

PEARSON

Scott Foresman

Editorial Offices: Glenview, Illinois • Parsippany, New Jersey • New York, New York
Sales Offices: Boston, Massachusetts • Duluth, Georgia • Glenview, Illinois
Coppell, Texas • Sacramento, California • Mesa, Arizona

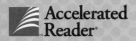

About the Cover Artist

When Scott Gustafson was in grade school, he spent most of his spare time drawing pictures. Now he gets to make pictures for a living. Before he starts a painting, he photographs his family, pets, or friends posing as characters that will appear in the illustration. He then uses the photos to inspire the finished picture. In this cover you can see his pet cockatiel, Piper.

ISBN-13: 978-0-328-24348-8
ISBN-10:   0-328-24348-5

2 3 4 5 6 7 8 9 10 V063 16 15 14 13 12 11 10 09 08 07
CC:N1

Dear Reader,

A new school year is beginning. Are you ready? You are about to take a trip along a famous street—*Scott Foresman Reading Street.* During this trip you will travel in space with some astronauts. You will explore the desert. You will go camping with Henry and his big dog Mudge. You will even build a robot with good friends Pearl and Wagner.

As you read these stories and articles, you will learn new things that will help you in science and social studies.

While you are enjoying these exciting pieces of literature, you will find that something else is going on—you are becoming a better reader.

Have a great trip, and don't forget to write!

Sincerely,
The Authors

Exploration

What can we learn from exploring new places and things?

4

Working Together

How can we work together?

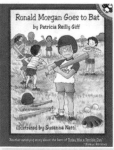

Creative Ideas

What does it mean to be creative?

Exploration

What can we learn from exploring new places and things?

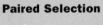

Let's Talk About
EXPLORATION

Words to Read

country
beautiful
front
someone
somewhere
friend

Read the Words

Iris and her family have moved to the country. It is a beautiful place. Iris looked at the long road in front of her house. She hopes that someone out there somewhere is waiting to be her friend.

Iris and Walter

Genre: Realistic Fiction

Realistic fiction is a made-up story that could happen in real life. Now read about Iris, a girl who moves to the country and finds a new friend.

Iris and Walter

by Elissa Haden Guest

illustrated by Christine Davenier

What new things does Iris learn
when she moves to the country?

A Walk and a Talk

Iris and Grandpa went for a walk.

"Can I tell you something?" Iris asked.

"You can tell me anything," said Grandpa.

"I hate the country," said Iris.

"Why?" asked Grandpa.

"Because there are no children here," said Iris. "The country is as lonely as Mars."

"Iris, my girl, there must be some children somewhere," said Grandpa.

"Do you think so?" asked Iris.

"I know so. We shall have to find them, Iris. We shall be explorers!"

Iris and Grandpa walked
down the road. The birds
were singing. The roses were
blooming. And around the
bend, someone was waiting.

Iris and Grandpa walked around the bend. They saw a great big green tree.

"What a tree!" said Grandpa.

"So green!" said Iris.

"So beautiful," said Grandpa.

"I want to climb it," said Iris.

Down came a ladder.

23

"Amazing! I wonder what's up there?" said Grandpa.

"I'll go see," said Iris. Iris began to climb.

"How is it up there?" called Grandpa.

"It's very green!" yelled Iris.

Iris climbed higher and higher until she was almost at the top of the great big green tree.

24

"Grandpa?!" called Iris.
"There's a house up here."
"Amazing!" said Grandpa.

Iris knocked on the door.

"Come in," said a voice.

Iris opened the door.

"Hi, I'm Walter," said Walter.

"I'm Iris," said Iris.

Iris and Walter shook hands.

"Hey, Grandpa, there's a kid up here named Walter!" yelled Iris.

"How wonderful," said Grandpa.

And it was.

A New Life

Iris and Walter played every day. They climbed trees. They rolled down hills. They played hide-and-seek.

When it rained,
Walter showed Iris his
hat collection. And Iris
showed Walter how to
roller-skate–indoors.

Some days they rode
Walter's sweet pony, Sal.
Other days they sat on a fence
and watched a horse named
Rain running wild.

"Tell me about the big city," said Walter.

"Well," said Iris, "in the big city, there are lots and lots and lots of people."

"Ah," said Walter. "But in the country there are lots and lots and lots of stars."

Iris and Walter played every day. But still Iris dreamed of the big city. She dreamed of her noisy street and her wide front stoop.

She dreamed of tango music and of
roller-skating down long hallways.
But Iris was not sad.

For in the country, there were
red-tailed hawks and starry skies.

There were pale roses. And there was
cool grass beneath her feet. There was a
wild horse named Rain and a sweet pony
named Sal.

And across the meadow,
over the stream, high in a tree,
was a little house. And inside
there was a new friend. . . Walter.

Think and Share

Talk About It Stories can go on and on. What do you think Iris and Walter do next?

1. Use the pictures below to retell the story. **Retell**

2. Where does *Iris and Walter* take place? How might the story be different if Iris and Walter had met in the city? **Character/Setting**

3. What did you predict Iris would find in the tree? Were you right? What other predictions did you make? **Predict**

Look Back and Write Look back at page 19. What problem did Iris have? How did that change? Use details from the story to help you.

Meet the Author and the Illustrator
Elissa Haden Guest

STARRING
ELISSA HADEN GUEST

Elissa Haden Guest likes big cities. She says, "New York was a very exciting place to grow up. You can walk for miles there without getting tired or bored because there's so much to see. Many of the streets are crowded with people and there's this terrific energy in the air."

Read more books about Iris and Walter.

Christine Davenier

Christine Davenier lives in France, where she grew up. She taught kindergarten for four years before attending art school. She has illustrated many children's books.

Morning Song

by Bobbi Katz

Today is a day to catch tadpoles.
Today is a day to explore.
Today is a day to get started.
Come on! Let's not sleep anymore.

Outside the sunbeams are dancing.
The leaves sing a rustling song.
Today is a day for adventures,
and I hope that you'll come along!

My Travel Tree

by Bobbi Katz

There are oh-so-many
kinds of trees—
apple, pear, pine—
but there is just one special tree
I feel is somehow mine.
Its branches form
such cozy nooks
for dreaming dreams
and reading books.
I sail to almost anywhere,
perched among the leaves up there.
If naming things were up to me,
I'd call this one my travel tree.

Write Now

Plan

Prompt

In *Iris and Walter,* Iris visits a treehouse and makes a friend. Think about a place you would like to visit.
Now write a plan that tells what you will see and do there.

Student Model

Place is named at beginning.

Writer lists things to do and see.

Voice shows how writer feels.

- I plan to visit Chicago.
- I will see many tall buildings.
- I will see busy streets with people.
- I will ride on the train.
- I will go to the zoo.
- It will be an exciting trip.

Sentences

A **sentence** is a group of words that tells a complete idea. The words are in an order that makes sense. A sentence begins with a capital letter. Many sentences end with a **period (.).**

Iris and Walter went swimming.

This is a sentence. It tells a complete idea.

· ·

Look at the sentences in the plan. How do you know they are sentences?

Let's Talk About

EXPLORATION

43

Words to Read

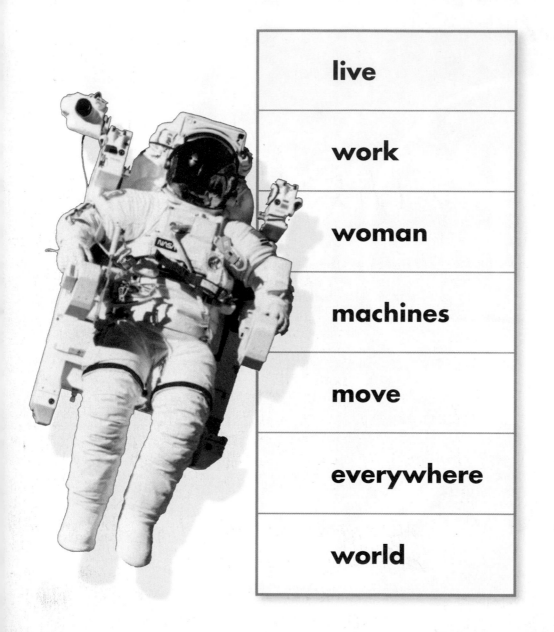

live
work
woman
machines
move
everywhere
world

Read the Words

Astronauts live and work in space.
A woman can be an astronaut.

Machines in space
can move
large things.

Stars are everywhere.
Can you see our world?

Genre: Expository Nonfiction
Expository nonfiction tells facts about a topic. Next you will read facts about the crew of a real space shuttle.

Exploring Space

with an Astronaut

by Patricia J. Murphy

What will you find out about space from an astronaut?

Lift-off!

3 . . . 2 . . . 1 . . . Lift-off!
A space shuttle climbs high into the sky. Inside the shuttle, astronauts are on their way to learn more about space.

What is an astronaut?

An astronaut is a person who goes into space. Astronauts fly on a space shuttle.

The space shuttle takes off like a rocket. It lands like an airplane.

United States

Meet Eileen Collins.

Eileen Collins is an astronaut. She was the first woman to be a space shuttle pilot. She was also the first woman to be the leader of a space shuttle trip.

She and four other astronauts worked as a team. Some astronauts flew the space shuttle. Others did experiments.

How do astronauts live in space?

In the space shuttle, astronauts float everywhere. Sleeping bags are tied to walls. Toilets have a type of seat belt.

Astronauts exercise to stay strong. They take sponge baths to keep clean.

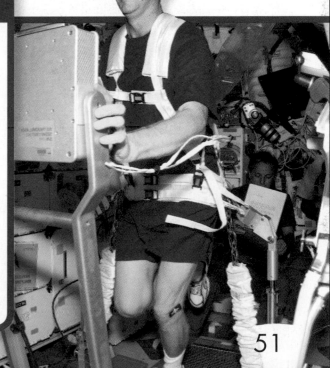

51

Why do astronauts go into space?

Astronauts test ways to live and work in a world that is very different from Earth. In space, there is no up and down, no air, and the sun always shines.

Astronauts do experiments. They look for problems and fix them. This will make space travel safer.

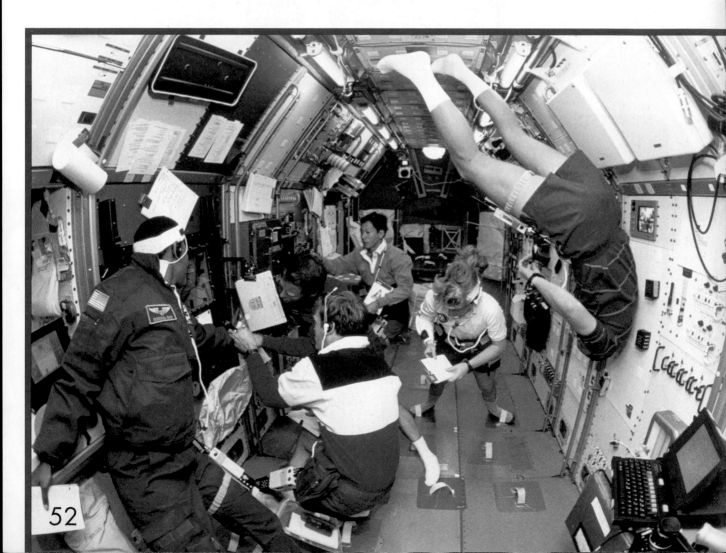

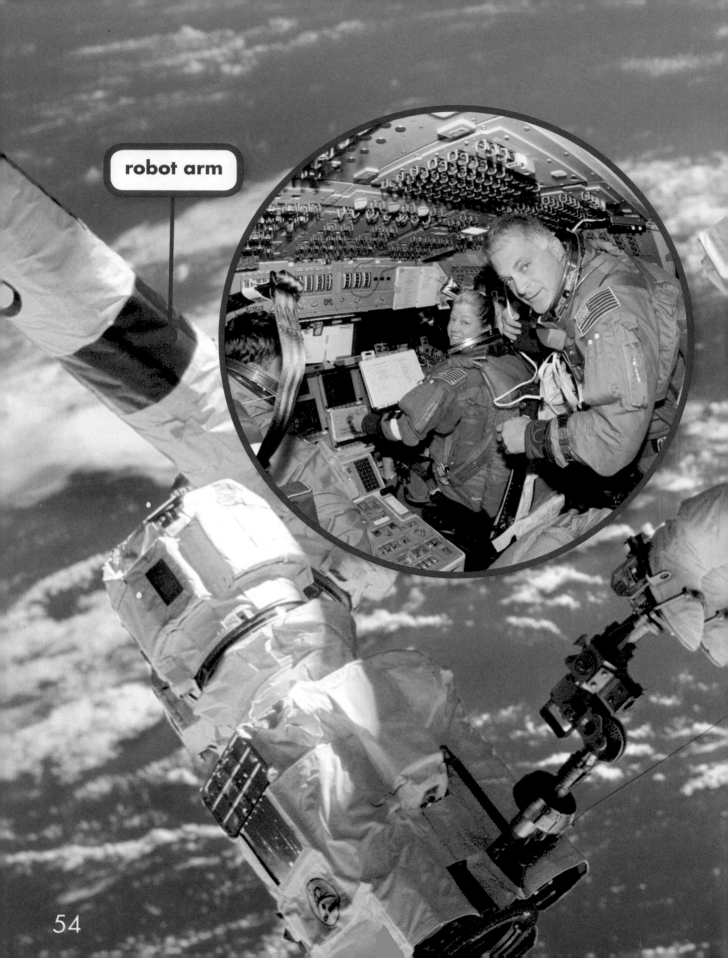

robot arm

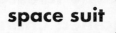

space suit

What tools do astronauts use?

A space shuttle is a giant toolbox! It holds tools, such as computers, that help fly the space shuttle.

Astronauts use robot arms to move things and people outside the shuttle. On space walks, space suits keep astronauts safe.

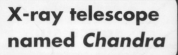

X-ray telescope named *Chandra*

X-ray telescope

space shuttle

The crew's special job

Eileen Collins and her crew had a special job to do. They took an X-ray telescope into space with them.

First, they tested the telescope. Next, they flipped some switches and let the telescope go into space. Then, the telescope used its rockets to fly higher into space.

Did the astronauts do other jobs, too?

Yes. They did experiments with plants and exercise machines. They were studying life without gravity.

When there was some time to rest, the astronauts could look out their window. They saw Earth from many, many miles away!

Rocky Mountains in Colorado

plant experiment

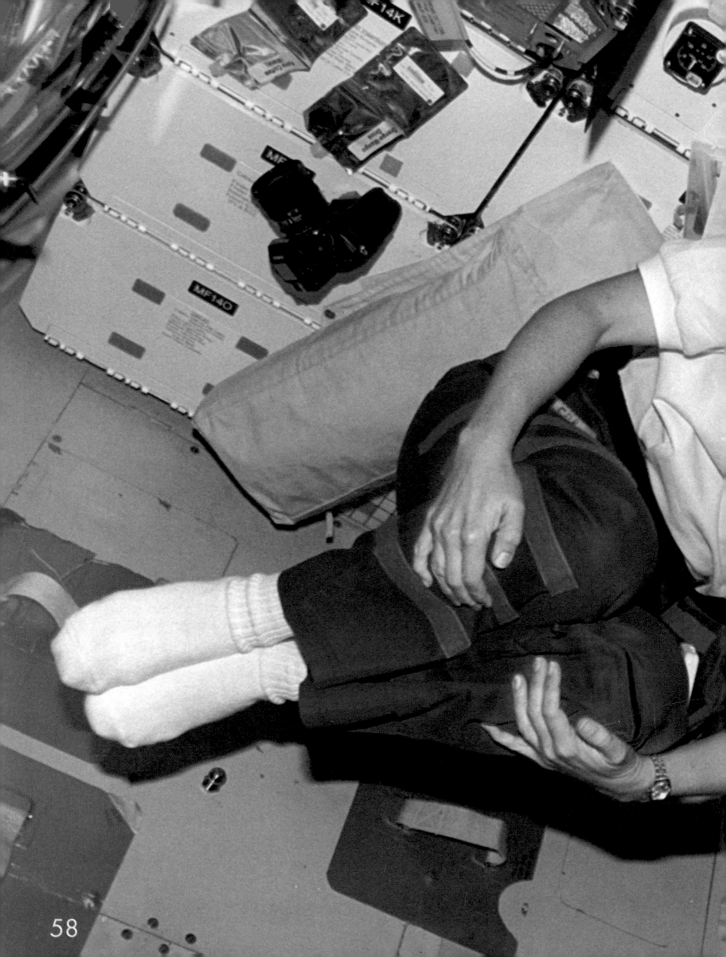

Would you like to fly into space?

Do you like math and science? Do you like to visit new places? Do you like fast roller coasters? Astronauts do, too! Maybe someday you will become an astronaut, just like Eileen Collins.

59

Think and Share

Talk About It You are an astronaut. Send a one-minute message to Earth. Tell about your trip.

1. Use the pictures below to summarize what you read about astronauts. **Retell**

2. What do you think is the most important thing the author wanted you to know? **Main Idea**

3. Most sections of this selection begin with a question. The next part answers the question. How did that format help you as you read? **Text Structure**

Look Back and Write If you really want to be an astronaut, what things should you like? Look back on page 59 to help you answer.

Meet the Author
Patricia J. Murphy

Patricia Murphy likes everything about writing a book. When she starts a new book, she says, it's "fun and scary." When she's in the middle, her days are filled with "unexpected adventure and surprises—and a lot of mess and hard work." In the end, when the book is written, she feels excited and a little sad that it's all over. Then it's on to the next book!

Ms. Murphy is a writer and a photographer. She lives in Illinois.

Read more books by Patricia Murphy.

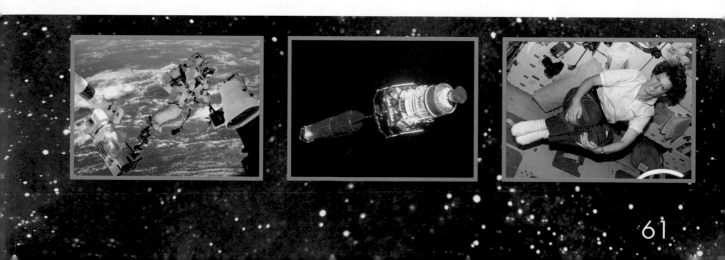

A Trip to Space Camp

by Ann Weil

What does it feel
like to go into space?
Would you like to find
out? Then maybe Space
Camp is for you!

There are all sorts of space camps that you could try. Some are for adults. Some are for teens. There is even a Space Camp for children as young as 7 years old. It is called Parent-Child Space Camp. Parent-Child Space Camp takes place over a long weekend. Families can go to Space Camp together.

Space Camp uses some of the same machines used to train real astronauts. There's a special chair that makes you feel like you are walking on the moon. Another chair is like the kind that astronauts use when they go outside their rocket ship to fix something. A third kind of chair makes you feel like you're floating in space. Still another machine spins you in circles and flips you head over heels. Then there's the Space Shot. The Space Shot shoots you straight into the air at about 45 to 50 miles per hour. You fall back down just as fast. Then you bump up and down a few times before it's over.

Y6 Gravity Chair

Working in Space

A Multi-Axis Giro

Everyone at space camp works together on special missions. On these missions you'll do work like real astronauts do in space. You might get to fly a rocket ship. It's only pretend, of course. You won't really fly into space. But it looks and feels like the real thing. And that's really fun!

Moon Gravity Chair

Write Now

Writing and Grammar

List

Prompt

Exploring Space with an Astronaut tells about astronauts. Think about astronauts' jobs in space. Now write a list of sentences that tell what they do.

Writing Trait

Good **word choice** makes your list interesting to read.

Student Model

Bullets separate items on list.

Each item on list is a sentence.

Writer <u>chooses</u> clear <u>words</u> to explain tasks.

- Astronauts exercise to keep fit.
- Some astronauts pilot shuttles.
- Some astronauts do experiments.
- Many astronauts repair things.
- Astronauts walk in space.
- Astronauts enjoy a great view of Earth.

Subjects

The **subject** of a sentence tells who or what does something.

An astronaut goes into space.

An astronaut is the subject of this sentence.

• •

Look at the sentences in the list. Write the subject of each sentence.

Let's Talk About
Exploration

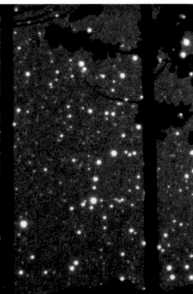

Words to Read

love

mother

father

straight

bear

couldn't

build

Read the Words

We all love camping. My mother and father take us camping every year. We go straight to the woods when we get there. Something new always happens on these trips. Last year, we saw a bear! I couldn't believe it. This year, my dad promised to teach us how to build a campfire. I can't wait!

Genre: Realistic Fiction Realistic fiction means that a story could happen. Next read about Henry and his dog, Mudge, and their camping trip.

Henry and Mudge

and the Starry Night

by Cynthia Rylant
illustrated by Suçie Stevenson

What will Henry and Mudge
find on a starry night?

Contents

Big Bear Lake

In August Henry and Henry's big
dog Mudge always went camping.
They went with Henry's parents.

Henry's mother had been a Camp Fire Girl, so she knew all about camping.

She knew how to set up a tent.

She knew how to build a campfire. She
knew how to cook camp food.

Henry's dad didn't
know anything about
camping. He just
came with a guitar
and a smile.

Henry and Mudge loved camping. This year they were going to Big Bear Lake, and Henry couldn't wait.

"We'll see deer, Mudge," Henry said.
Mudge wagged.

"We'll see raccoons," said Henry.
Mudge shook Henry's hand.

"We might even see a *bear*," Henry said. Henry was not so sure he wanted to see a bear. He shivered and put an arm around Mudge.

Mudge gave a big, slow, *loud* yawn. He drooled on Henry's foot. Henry giggled. "No bear will get *us*, Mudge," Henry said. "We're too *slippery!*"

A Good Smelly Hike

Henry and Mudge and Henry's parents drove
to Big Bear Lake. They parked the car and got
ready to hike.

Everyone had a backpack, even Mudge.
(His had lots of crackers.) Henry's mother said,
"Let's go!" And off they went.

They walked and walked and climbed and
climbed. It was beautiful.

Henry saw a fish jump straight out of a stream.
He saw a doe and her fawn. He saw waterfalls
and a rainbow.

Mudge didn't see much of anything. He was smelling. Mudge loved to hike and smell. He smelled a raccoon from yesterday. He smelled a deer from last night.

He smelled an oatmeal cookie from Henry's back pocket. "Mudge!" Henry laughed, giving Mudge the cookie.

Finally Henry's mother picked a good place to camp.

Henry's parents set up the tent. Henry
unpacked the food and pans and lanterns. Mudge
unpacked a ham sandwich. Finally the camp was
almost ready. It needed just one more thing:
"Who knows the words to 'Love Me Tender'?"
said Henry's father with a smile, pulling out his
guitar. Henry looked at Mudge and groaned.

Green Dreams

It was a beautiful night.

Henry and Henry's parents lay on their backs by the fire and looked at the sky. Henry didn't know there were so many stars in the sky.

"There's the Big Dipper," said Henry's mother.

"There's the Little Dipper," said Henry.

"There's E. T.," said Henry's dad.

Mudge wasn't looking at stars. He was chewing on a log. He couldn't get logs this good at home. Mudge loved camping.

Henry's father sang one more sappy love song, then everyone went inside the tent to sleep. Henry's father and mother snuggled. Henry and Mudge snuggled.

It was as quiet as quiet could be. Everyone slept safe and sound, and there were no bears, no scares. Just the clean smell of trees . . . and wonderful green dreams.

Think and Share

Talk About It Pretend you are Mudge. What were the best sights and smells on the camping trip?

1. Look at the pictures below. They are in the wrong order. Reorder them, then retell the story. **Retell**

2. Who are the characters in this story? Describe the setting. **Character/Setting**

3. Did anything in this story confuse you? What did you do about it? **Monitor and Fix Up**

Look Back and Write Look at pages 76 and 77. Who knew all about camping? What did that person do to help with the camping trip? Use details from the story.

Meet the Author and the Illustrator
Cynthia Rylant

Cynthia Rylant never read many books when she was young. There was no library in her town.

After college, Ms. Rylant worked in a library. "Within a few weeks, I fell in love with children's books," she says. She has written over 60 books!

Suçie Stevenson

Suçie Stevenson has drawn pictures for most of the Henry and Mudge books. Her brother's Great Dane, Jake, was her inspiration for Mudge.

Read more books by Cynthia Rylant.

CYNTHIA RYLANT
POPPLETON
Forever
Illustrated by MARK TEAGUE

CYNTHIA RYLANT
Mr. Putter & Tabby
Stir the Soup
Illustrated by
Arthur Howard

Star Pictures in the Sky

by Lorraine McCombs

Have you ever connected the dots to make a picture? Think about the stars in the sky. A long time ago, people saw the stars as dots in the night sky. They imagined lines going from star to star. They called these star pictures *constellations.*

On a very dark night away from the city, we can see hundreds of stars in the sky. We can even see the same constellations that people saw long ago. Here are a few of them.

This star picture, or constellation, is called Orion. It is named after a famous hunter in Greek stories. We see Orion best in the winter sky. This constellation has three stars in a row. They are thought of as Orion's belt.

The Big Dipper is a star picture in the constellation called Big Bear. We can see the Big Dipper any time of the year, but it is best seen between January and October. Two stars in the Big Dipper point toward the very bright North Star.

Orion's Belt

Orion

Big Dipper

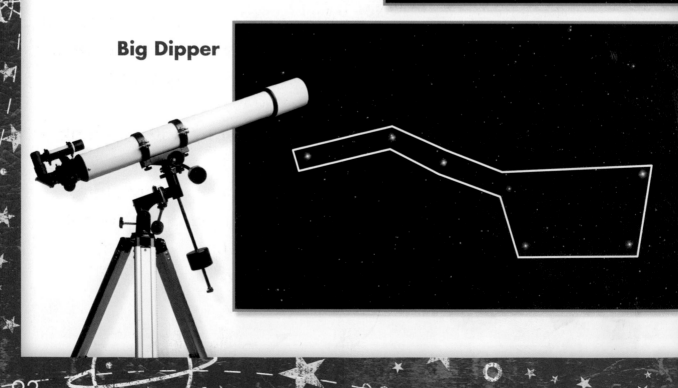

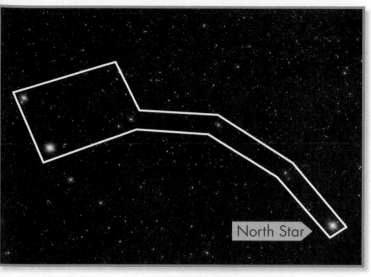

Little Dipper

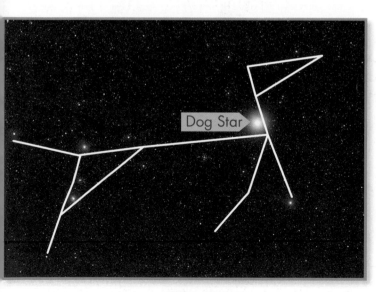

Big Dog

Another star picture is the Little Dipper. You can see the Little Dipper all year. Notice the handle. The brightest star in the handle is the North Star. It never moves. For hundreds of years, people have used the North Star to find their way.

Canis was a dog in Greek stories. *Canis* means "dog," and this constellation is known as the Big Dog. The very bright star is called the Dog Star. It is the brightest star in our whole nighttime sky. You can usually find this constellation in the summer sky between July and September.

The next time you look up at a dark, starry sky, think about these constellations. Connect the dots as people did long ago. What star pictures do you see?

Write Now

Writing and Grammar

Story

Prompt

In *Henry and Mudge,* a family camps in the woods.
Think about a fun outdoor place.
Now write a story that tells about something that happens at this place.

Writing Trait

Vivid **word choice** makes a picture for your readers.

Student Model

Topic is named in first sentence.

Luke goes to the beach on hot summer days. He splashes in the cool water. He digs in the warm sand. He finds smooth rocks and pretty seashells for a sand castle. Luke throws bread to the noisy gulls. They always want more.

Details tell about things Luke does.

Writer <u>chooses</u> strong, vivid <u>words</u>.

Writer's Checklist

✓ **Focus** Do all sentences tell about an outdoor place?

✓ **Organization** Are ideas in an order that makes sense?

✓ **Support** Does each detail add more information?

✓ **Conventions** Are punctuation and spelling correct?

Grammar

Predicates

The **predicate** tells what the subject of a sentence does or is.

Henry and Mudge **walked down the trail.**

The words **walked down the trail** tell what Henry and Mudge did.

• •

Look at the sentences in the beach story. Write the predicates of the first three sentences.

Let's Talk About
EXPLORATION

Words to Read

water
full
animals
early
warm
eyes

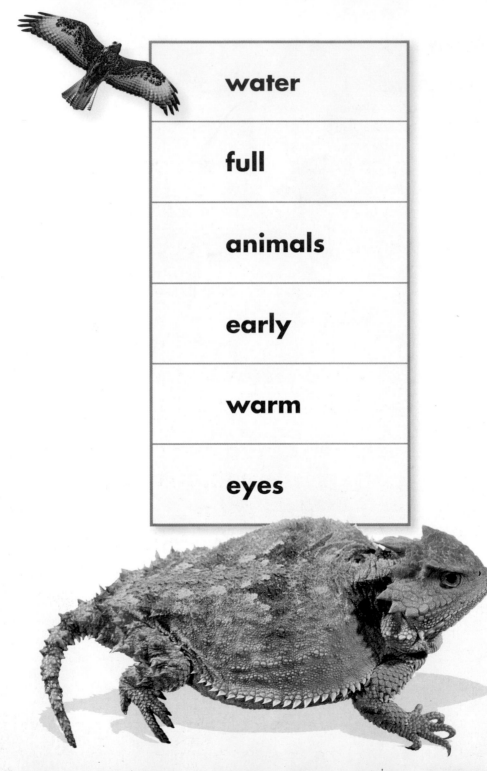

Read the Words

Some places on Earth have very little water. It is hot and dry, but these places are full of life. Plants and animals can live there. You can visit these places too. Go out early before the sun is too warm. Be sure to protect your eyes when you go out!

A Walk in the
Desert

Genre: Expository Nonfiction

Expository nonfiction gives information about a topic. In the next selection, you will read about a walk in the desert.

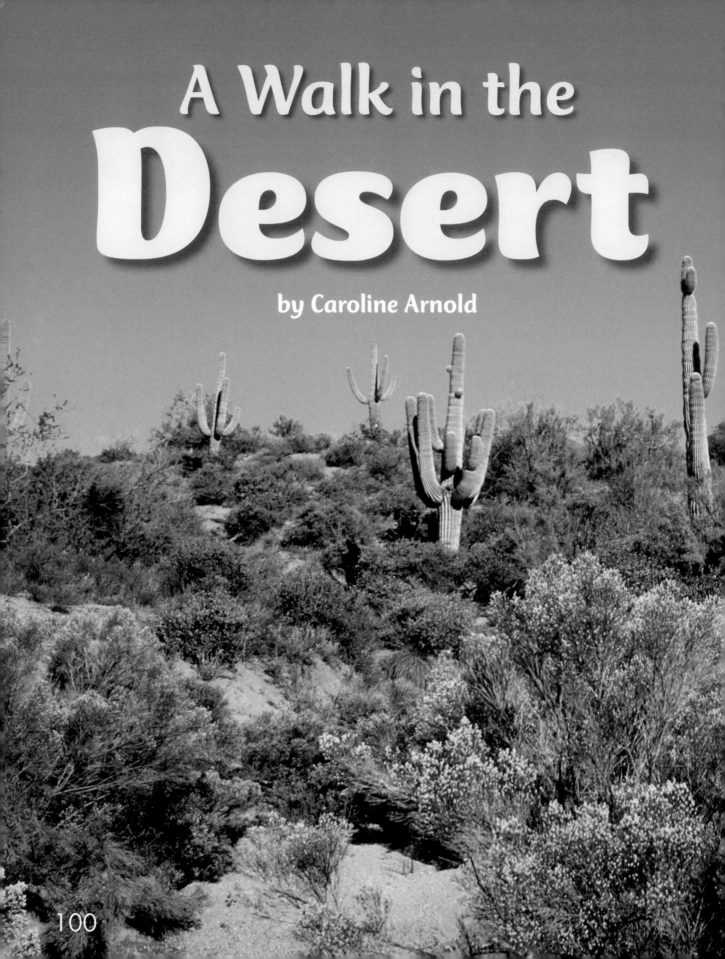

A Walk in the
Desert

by Caroline Arnold

What can you find on a walk in the desert?

See the bright sun. Feel the dry air. It is hot—very hot! Where are we?

We're in the desert. Let's take a walk and see what we can find.

The ground is dry in the desert. It almost never rains. With so little water, it is hard for anything to live. But many plants and animals make their home in this harsh climate. You just have to look closely to see them.

Hedgehog Cactus

Teddy-Bear Cholla Cactus

Cactus is one kind of plant that grows in the desert. It doesn't have leaves. Instead, it has sharp spines. The spines protect the cactus from animals who might want to eat it. A cactus stores water in its stem. It uses the water when there is no rain.

Prickly Pear Cactus

Barrel Cactus

Saguaro Cactus

Look up at the tall saguaro. It is a giant among cactus plants. It took many years to grow so tall.

In late spring, white flowers bloom. Birds and insects drink the flowers' sweet nectar. After the flowers die, a red fruit grows.

Prickly Pear Fruit

Saguaro Cactus with White Flowers

Hawk

The saguaro cactus is home to many desert creatures. *Tap, tap, tap,* pecks a woodpecker. It is carving a hole for its nest. Old holes become nests for other birds.

A hawk is searching for food below. Its sharp eyes can spot even a tiny mouse.

Woodpecker

Owl

What is that large bird? It's a roadrunner. *Coo, coo, coo,* it calls. The roadrunner hardly ever flies, but it can run fast. Watch it chase a lizard to eat.

Roadrunner

Tree Lizard

Here are some other lizards. Lizards need the sun's heat to warm their scaly bodies. But when it gets too hot, they look for shade.

Zebra-Tailed Lizard

Leopard Lizard

Short-Horned Lizard

A rattlesnake lies next to a rock. Its earth colors make it hard to see. Rattlesnakes are dangerous. A bite from one will kill a small animal. If you hear a rattlesnake shake its tail, it is trying to scare you away.

Look! Did you see that rock move? It isn't a rock at all. It's a desert tortoise. The hard shell protects the tortoise from enemies and from the hot sun. The tortoise uses its sharp beak to break off tough desert grasses. It sometimes eats cactus fruits, too.

Rattlesnake

Cactus Fruits

Desert Tortoise

The jack rabbit is also a plant eater. Watch it sniff the early evening air. It is alert to the sounds and smells of the desert. When danger is near, the jack rabbit's long legs help it to escape quickly.

Jack Rabbits

As night begins to fall, the desert air cools. Animals who were hidden or sleeping come out to hunt and feed. A hungry coyote howls to the moon.

Do you see the small kit fox? Big ears help the fox to hear well so it can track animals to eat.

The cool night is full of activity.

Kangaroo Rat

Small Kit Fox

Owl

Coyote

The desert is an exciting place to visit. You can ride a mule along a deep canyon, slide down a sand dune, learn about wildlife at a nature center, or taste sweet jelly made from prickly pear fruit.

Prickly Pear Fruit

Riding a mule

Sliding down a sand dune

You can find deserts all over the world. Not all deserts are alike. Some are hot. Others are cold. But in all deserts there is little rain.

North America

South America

The deserts in South America have very little animal or plant life.

The Gila monster is the only poisonous lizard in the American Desert.

The Gobi Desert is cold and snowy in the winter. Temperatures are often below freezing.

The tiny fennec fox lives in the world's largest desert—the Sahara.

Asia

Europe

Africa

The Australian Desert is home to the bandicoot.

Australia

The dromedary is a one-humped camel found in the sandy Arabian Desert.

Can you find the continent where you live?

Is there a desert on it?

119

Think and Share

Talk About It You and some friends go walking in the desert. Tell your friends what to look at and listen for.

1. Use the pictures below to summarize what you learned. **Retell**

2. Look back at the story to find details that tell about desert plants and animals. **Main Idea and Details**

3. The author wrote about the desert as if she were taking you for a walk. Find examples of that in the selection. How did that help you as you read? **Text Structure**

Look Back and Write Look at pages 116–117. What other things can you do in the desert?

120

Meet the Author
Caroline Arnold

Caroline Arnold has walked in several deserts in the southwestern United States. After she moved to California, she says, "I grew to love the desert."

Ms. Arnold is fascinated by the way living things adapt to the extreme heat and cold and the lack of water in the desert. "I get a thrill out of watching birds, squirrels, rabbits, coyotes, peccaries, lizards, and other desert animals when I spend time in the desert," she says.

Read two other books by Caroline Arnold.

A Walk By The Seashore
First Facts
Written by Caroline Arnold
Illustrated by Freya Tanz

SOUTH AMERICAN ANIMALS
CAROLINE ARNOLD

Rain Forests

Sammy read *A Walk in the Desert* and learned a lot. However, he knows that deserts are not everywhere. In fact, his home is near a forest. His family often goes there to fish, swim, and picnic. "But what exactly is a forest?" Sammy asks himself. To find out more, he goes to an online reference Web site.

Here Sammy finds four different sources: an atlas, an almanac, a dictionary, and an encyclopedia. Sammy clicks on Encyclopedia. Then he types the keyword *forest* into the search engine and clicks on "go." He gets a list of results that begins like this:

File   Edit   View   Favorites   Tools   Help

http://www.url.here

Search Results: forest

forest (encyclopedia)

forest, a dense growth of trees, together with other plants, covering a large area of land.

For more practice

Take It to the Net

PearsonSuccessNet.com

Sammy clicks on the forest link and finds an encyclopedia article. As he reads it, he finds a link to Types of Forests. This makes him curious. He clicks on Types of Forests and finds this information.

Types of Forests

You can find rain forests all over the world, including Central and South America and Central and West Africa. Parts of Asia and Australia also have rain forests. Rain forests get lots of rain every year—160–400 inches. The average temperature is 80°F. Many different kinds of plants and animals live in rain forests.

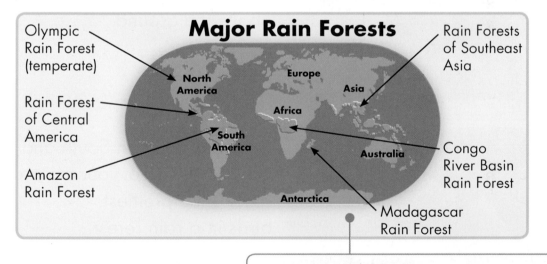

Major Rain Forests

Olympic Rain Forest (temperate)

Rain Forest of Central America

Amazon Rain Forest

North America

Europe

Asia

Africa

South America

Australia

Antarctica

Rain Forests of Southeast Asia

Congo River Basin Rain Forest

Madagascar Rain Forest

Sammy wonders where some of the countries with rain forests are. He uses the atlas on the Web site. He finds this map showing rain forests all over the world.

So far, Sammy has read part of an encyclopedia article and looked at a map. Sammy now goes back to the online reference Web site. He wants to find pictures of animals that live in rain forests. Sammy follows the steps and does another search. He finds these pictures on the Web site of a large university.

File   Edit   View   Favorites   Tools   Help

http://www.url.here

Trees are the foundation of the rain forest. This tree is *Pterocarpus*. Its roots grow above the ground.

Toucans live in South and Central America. Toucans are among the prettiest birds in a rain forest.

Some crocodiles grow to a very large size—up to twenty feet. But smaller ones (ten feet) are more usual.

Some native South Americans use the poison from poison dart frogs to make darts for hunting.

Sammy is so interested that he continues searching until he finds out all he needs to know about rain forests.

125

Write Now

Writing and Grammar

Report

Prompt

A Walk in the Desert tells about plants and animals in the desert.
Think about your neighborhood.
Now write a report about who and what live there.

Writing Trait

Conventions are rules for writing.

Student Model

Writer uses a question to create interest.

Who lives in my neighborhood?
People live in homes. Pet dogs and cats live there too. Flowers grow in the gardens. Trees grow near the streets. Squirrels and birds

Writer follows <u>conventions</u> for sentences.

live in the trees. **Many people and animals live in my neighborhood. Plants grow there too.**

Ending states main idea.

Grammar

Statements and Questions

A **statement** is a sentence that tells something. A statement ends with a **period (.)**.

The desert is dry**.**

A **question** is a sentence that asks something. A question ends with a **question mark (?)**.

Do you see the small kit fox**?**

. . . .

Write a statement and a question from the report. Circle the period and the question mark.

Let's Talk About
Exploration

Words to Read

pieces
often
very
together
though
gone
learn

Read the Words

Chip looked at the pieces of the puzzle. He often did these things with his very best friend Mike. He and Mike couldn't work together today, though. Mike had gone to visit his uncle. Chip knew he would have to learn to do things on his own.

Genre: Play

A play is a story written to be acted out for others. Next, you will read a play about an ant who sets out to learn who is the strongest one.

The Strongest One

retold as a play by Joseph Bruchac
illustrated by David Diaz
from *Pushing Up the Sky*

What does Little Red Ant
learn about being strong?

Characters:

NARRATOR

LITTLE RED ANT

SECOND ANT

THIRD ANT

FOURTH ANT

SNOW

SUN

WIND

HOUSE

MOUSE

CAT

STICK

FIRE

WATER

DEER

ARROW

BIG ROCK

Scene I: Inside the Ant's Hole

(On a darkened stage, the ants crouch together.)

NARRATOR: Little Red Ant lived in a hole under the Big Rock with all of its relatives. It often wondered about the world outside: Who in the world was the strongest one of all? One day in late spring Little Red Ant decided to find out.

LITTLE RED ANT: I am going to find out who is strongest. I am going to go outside and walk around.

SECOND ANT: Be careful! We ants are very small. Something might step on you.

THIRD ANT: Yes, we are the smallest and weakest ones of all.

FOURTH ANT: Be careful, it is dangerous out there!

LITTLE RED ANT: I will be careful. I will find out who is strongest. Maybe the strongest one can teach us how to be stronger.

Scene II: The Mesa

(Ant walks back and forth onstage.)

NARRATOR: So Little Red Ant went outside and began to walk around. But as Little Red Ant walked, the snow began to fall.

(Snow walks onstage.)

LITTLE RED ANT: Ah, my feet are cold. This snow makes everything freeze. Snow must be the strongest. I will ask. Snow, are you the strongest of all?

SNOW: No, I am not the strongest.

LITTLE RED ANT: Who is stronger than you?

SNOW: Sun is stronger. When Sun shines on me, I melt away. Here it comes!

(As Sun walks onstage, Snow hurries offstage.)

LITTLE RED ANT: Ah, Sun must be the strongest. I will ask. Sun, are you the strongest of all?

SUN: No, I am not the strongest.

LITTLE RED ANT: Who is stronger than you?

SUN: Wind is stronger. Wind blows the clouds across the sky and covers my face. Here it comes!

(As Wind comes onstage, Sun hurries offstage with face covered in hands.)

LITTLE RED ANT: Wind must be the strongest. I will ask. Wind, are you the strongest of all?

WIND: No, I am not the strongest.

LITTLE RED ANT: Who is stronger than you?

WIND: House is stronger. When I come to House, I cannot move it. I must go elsewhere. Here it comes!

(As House walks onstage, Wind hurries offstage.)

LITTLE RED ANT: House must be the strongest. I will ask. House, are you the strongest of all?

HOUSE: No, I am not the strongest.

LITTLE RED ANT: Who is stronger than you?

HOUSE: Mouse is stronger. Mouse comes and gnaws holes in me. Here it comes!

(As Mouse walks onstage, House hurries offstage.)

LITTLE RED ANT: Mouse must be the strongest. I will ask. Mouse, are you the strongest of all?

MOUSE: No, I am not the strongest.

LITTLE RED ANT: Who is stronger than you?

MOUSE: Cat is stronger. Cat chases me, and if Cat catches me, Cat will eat me. Here it comes!

(As Cat walks onstage, Mouse hurries offstage, squeaking.)

LITTLE RED ANT: Cat must be the strongest. I will ask. Cat, are you the strongest of all?

CAT: No, I am not the strongest.

LITTLE RED ANT: Who is stronger than you?

CAT: Stick is stronger. When Stick hits me, I run away. Here it comes!

(As Stick walks onstage, Cat hurries offstage, meowing.)

LITTLE RED ANT: Stick must be the strongest. I will ask. Stick, are you the strongest of all?

STICK: No, I am not the strongest.

LITTLE RED ANT: Who is stronger than you?

STICK: Fire is stronger. When I am put into Fire, Fire burns me up! Here it comes!

(As Fire walks onstage, Stick hurries offstage.)

LITTLE RED ANT: Fire must be the strongest. I will ask. Fire, are you the strongest of all?

FIRE: No, I am not the strongest.

LITTLE RED ANT: Who is stronger than you?

FIRE: Water is stronger. When Water is poured on me, it kills me. Here it comes!

(As Water walks onstage, Fire hurries offstage.)

LITTLE RED ANT: Water must be the strongest. I will ask. Water, are you the strongest of all?

WATER: No, I am not the strongest.

LITTLE RED ANT: Who is stronger than you?

WATER: Deer is stronger. When Deer comes, Deer drinks me. Here it comes!

(As Deer walks onstage, Water hurries offstage.)

LITTLE RED ANT: Deer must be the strongest. I will ask. Deer, are you the strongest of all?

DEER: No, I am not the strongest.

LITTLE RED ANT: Who is stronger than you?

DEER: Arrow is stronger. When Arrow strikes me, it can kill me. Here it comes!

(As Arrow walks onstage, Deer runs offstage with leaping bounds.)

LITTLE RED ANT: Arrow must be the strongest. I will ask. Arrow, are you the strongest of all?

ARROW: No, I am not the strongest.

LITTLE RED ANT: Who is stronger than you?

ARROW: Big Rock is stronger. When I am shot from the bow and I hit Big Rock, Big Rock breaks me.

LITTLE RED ANT: Do you mean the same Big Rock where the Red Ants live?

ARROW: Yes, that is Big Rock. Here it comes!

(As Big Rock walks onstage, Arrow runs offstage.)

LITTLE RED ANT: Big Rock must be the strongest. I will ask. Big Rock, are you the strongest of all?

BIG ROCK: No, I am not the strongest.

LITTLE RED ANT: Who is stronger than you?

BIG ROCK: You are stronger. Every day you and the other Red Ants come and carry little pieces of me away. Someday I will be gone.

Scene III: The Ant's Hole

NARRATOR: So Little Red Ant went back home and spoke to the ant people.

(The ants crouch together on the darkened stage.)

SECOND ANT: Little Red Ant has returned.

THIRD ANT: He has come back alive!

FOURTH ANT: Tell us about what you have learned. Who is the strongest of all?

LITTLE RED ANT: I have learned that everything is stronger than something else. And even though we ants are small, in some ways we are the strongest of all.

149

Think and Share

Talk About It You could do this play as a dance or a puppet show. Tell how.

1. Use the pictures below to retell the story. On another piece of paper, draw more pictures to show the missing parts. **Retell**

2. Is *The Strongest One* a realistic story or a fantasy? What makes it so? **Realism and Fantasy**

3. How is a play different from other selections? How did that change the way you read it? **Monitor and Fix Up**

Look Back and Write Look back at page 135. Why does Little Red Ant want to find the strongest one? Use details from the selection in your answer.

Meet the Author
Joseph Bruchac

As a child, Joseph Bruchac loved to explore nature— the animals, birds, insects, and plants around him. His grandfather, an Abenaki Indian, taught him many things about nature.

Today, Mr. Bruchac tells traditional Native American stories. "In the Abenaki Indian tradition," he says, "there is a story connected to just about every bird, animal, and plant." One message in many of these tales is that all parts of nature are important. Even tiny ants can make a difference!

Read more books by Joseph Bruchac.

ANTEATERS

by John Jacobs

Have you ever heard of an anteater? Have you ever seen one? Let's learn more about them.

South America

Where do they live?

Anteaters live mostly in South and Central America where there are lots of grasses, swamps, and rain forests. These are the kinds of places where many ants live. Anteaters explore these grasses, swamps, and rain forests all day looking for ants to eat.

What do they look like?

The giant anteater, which is the most common, looks like nothing you've ever seen before. It has a bushy tail and a fat body. It has a tiny mouth, small eyes, and small ears. Its most important body parts are its sharp claws and its long, long tongue. (Its tongue is almost two feet long. That's as long as two rulers put together!)

How do they eat?

An anteater looks for ants by smelling the ground. When it finds an ants' nest, the anteater breaks it open with its sharp claws. It puts its long tongue down into the nest. Ants stick to the tongue and the anteater swallows them. The anteater does this over and over very fast until it is full. The anteater eats only a small number of ants at a time from any one nest. It does not want to run out of food! But ants, beware! It will return.

Write Now

News Report

Prompt

The Strongest One is a play with animals that talk.
Think about what it would be like to discover a talking animal.
Now write a news report about it.

Writing Trait

Different kinds of **sentences** make writing smoother.

Student Model

Events are told in order they happened.

Exclamation shows writer's feelings.

Writer uses different kinds of sentences.

A talking raccoon appeared in my yard today. It was sitting next to a bush. It said, "Hi, my name is Rusty. Can I have a snack?" I could not believe my ears! "Wait right here, Rusty." When I came back, Rusty was gone. No other neighbors saw him.

156

Grammar

Commands and Exclamations

A **command** is a sentence that tells someone to do something. It usually ends with a **period (.).**

Be careful out there**.**

An **exclamation** is a sentence that shows surprise or strong feeling. It ends with an **exclamation mark (!).**

I am excited**!**

· ·

Write a command and an exclamation from the news report. Circle the period and the exclamation mark.

A Postcard from My Explorations

connect to

WRITING

Which place did you read about that you would most like to explore? Imagine that you are there. Write a postcard to a friend. Tell about what you learned from exploring this place. Add a picture to your postcard.

It's amazing! The country is so different from the city. I didn't like it at first.

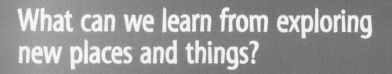

The Strongest One

connect to
SCIENCE

In *The Strongest One*, an ant discovers that it, too, is strong. Think about things in nature. Are some things stronger than others? Make a list. Include yourself on the list. Put the list in order, from the strongest to the weakest. Then make a graph with pictures and labels. Show the strongest, the weakest, and everything in between.

| weakest | —————————— | strongest |

sun
me
rain
squirrel
dog
bee
snow

Comparing Surroundings

connect to
SOCIAL STUDIES

In this unit, you read about many different places that people can explore. Choose two places that are very different. Make a Venn diagram. Tell how the places are different. Tell how they are alike.

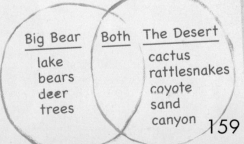

Big Bear / Both / The Desert

lake
bears
deer
trees

cactus
rattlesnakes
coyote
sand
canyon

159

Working Together

How can we work together?

Tara and Tiree, Fearless Friends

Faithful pets work together
to save a life.

REALISTIC FICTION

connect to
SOCIAL
STUDIES

Ronald Morgan Goes to Bat

Ronald provides his team
with spirit.

REALISTIC FICTION

connect to
SOCIAL
STUDIES

Turtle's Race with Beaver

Beaver learns the importance
of cooperation.

FOLK TALE

connect to
SCIENCE

The Bremen Town Musicians

Animals work together
to stop the robbers.

FAIRY TALE

connect to
SCIENCE

A Turkey for Thanksgiving

The animals work together to
make a happy Thanksgiving.

ANIMAL FANTASY

connect to
SOCIAL
STUDIES

Let's Talk About
Working Together

Words to Read

family
pull
listen
once
heard
break

Read the Words

   Tag is our family pet. He is a good dog. He will pull on my pants leg until I take him for a walk. He will listen and do what I say. Once he heard me call and came running so fast that I thought he would break a leg.

Genre: Realistic Fiction
Realistic fiction has made-up characters that act like real people and animals. Next you will read a story about two dogs that saved their owner.

Tara and Tiree,
Fearless Friends

by Andrew Clements
illustrated by Scott Gustafson

What makes Tara and Tiree fearless friends?

When Jim was a boy in Canada, his family had dogs. Jim loved those dogs. They were like part of his family.

When Jim grew up, he still loved dogs. He learned how to train them. He helped dogs learn to be good.

He always said, "There is no such thing as a bad dog." Training dogs became Jim's job.

Jim had two dogs named Tara and Tiree.
Tara was mostly black. Tiree was mostly gold.
Jim loved them both, and they loved him too.
Jim and his dogs liked the winter time.

They had good coats to keep warm. They
played in the snow. They went for long walks.

They liked going out, but they liked going back
in too. It was good to sit by the fire and listen to
the wind.

Jim's house was by a lake. Every winter there was ice on it. One day Jim went for a walk out on the lake. Tara and Tiree went too. The dogs loved to run across the ice.

It was very cold. Jim was ready to go back home. Then all at once the ice broke. Jim fell into the cold, cold water.

Jim called for help. No one was near. No one could hear him. But Tara and Tiree heard Jim and came running. Jim wanted the dogs to stay away. He was afraid for them.

But Tiree loved Jim. She wanted to help.
When she came near the hole, the ice broke again.
Tiree fell into the water with Jim.

The water was so cold. Jim knew he did not
have much time. Jim tried to help Tiree get out.
But the ice broke more and more.

Jim hoped Tara would run away. He did not want her to fall in the water too. But Tara did not run away. She wanted to help.

First Tara got down low. Then she came closer, little by little. The ice did not break.

Jim put out his hand. Tara got very close. Then Jim got hold of Tara's collar. Jim held on. Tara pulled back, but Jim was too big. He was still in the cold water.

Then Tiree did something very smart. She walked on Jim's back—up and out of the water! Tiree was cold, but she was safe! Did she run off the ice? No. She loved Jim too much to run away.

Tiree got down on her belly like Tara. She got close to Jim. Jim held out his other hand. And he grabbed on to Tiree's collar!

The two dogs pulled back hard. They slipped, but they didn't stop. Slowly they pulled Jim up onto the ice. He was safe.

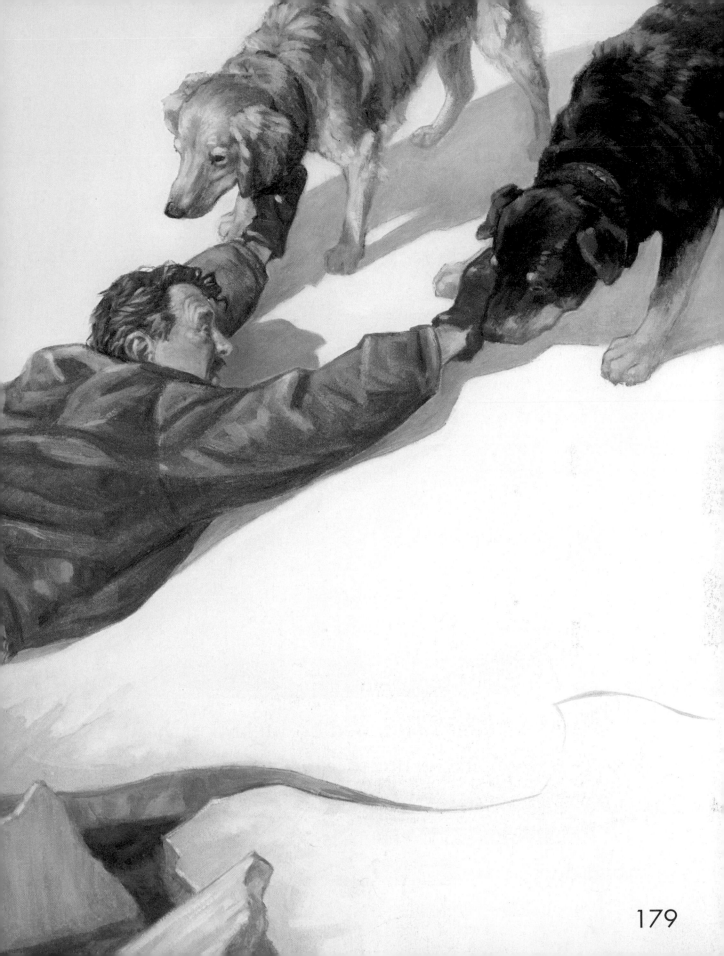

Tara and Tiree had saved his life! Soon they were all back in the house. They sat by the fire until they were warm again.

Jim always said, "There is no such thing as a bad dog."

Now Jim says something else too: "There *is* such a thing as a brave and wonderful dog!"

Jim is sure of this, because he has two of them—Tara and Tiree.

Think and Share

Talk About It Choose the most exciting part of this story. What makes it exciting? Read it.

1. Use the pictures below to retell the story. **Retell**

2. Tara seemed to know what to do when Jim fell into the water. What did she do first? What happened next? **Sequence**

3. What did you predict would happen to Jim? Were you right? What other predictions did you make? **Predict**

Look Back and Write Look back at pages 176–177. Tiree did something smart and something kind. What did she do? Use details from the selection in your answer.

Meet the Author
Andrew Clements

Andrew Clements says, "Every good writer I know started off as a good reader." When he was growing up, he loved to read. He remembers a school librarian who made him feel he was the "owner" of every book he read. He says, "That's one of the greatest things about reading a book—read it, and you own it forever."

Mr. Clements once taught school. Because he believes books make a difference, he read to his students in the classroom and to his four sons at home.

Read two more books by Andrew Clements.

Rescue Dogs

by Rena Moran

Do you know that dogs can be trained to save lives? These dogs are called rescue dogs. When people are in danger, rescue dogs are ready to help them.

Whom do they help?

Rescue dogs find lost hikers and campers. They find people who are trapped after an earthquake or an avalanche. When people get lost in a snowstorm, rescue dogs search for them. Some dogs can even save people from drowning.

What kinds of dogs make good rescue dogs?

Good rescue dogs must be strong and smart. They also must listen to the people who train and handle them. Saint Bernards have been working as rescue dogs for many years. They help rescue people who get lost in snowstorms or get trapped under deep snow.

Bloodhounds, Labrador retrievers, and German shepherds are good at following the trails of lost people. German shepherds also are good at finding people who are trapped under snow. Newfoundlands do a great job with water rescues.

How do they do their jobs?

Like all dogs, rescue dogs have a very good sense of smell. They use their sense of smell to find a lost person. First, the dog sniffs something with the person's scent on it. This could be a hat or a blanket. Then, the dog follows the scent trail the person has left.

Rescue dogs do not always look for just one person. Often, they try to find the scent of any person in a certain spot. This is useful when more than one person is lost.

Of course, rescue dogs could not do their jobs without the people who train and handle them. Who are these people? Most of them are people who love working with dogs. They also like to help rescue people who are in danger—just like their dogs do!

Write Now

Writing and Grammar

Directions

Prompt

In *Tara and Tiree,* two dogs save the life of their owner, Jim.
Think about the steps the dogs took to save Jim's life.
Now write directions that describe the steps you take to make or do something.

Writing Trait

Organize your steps in order, from first to last.

Student Model

First sentence tells what is made.

> Create a tasty sandwich. First, spread peanut butter on one slice of bread. Then sprinkle raisins on the peanut butter. Next, spread honey on another slice of bread. Finally, press the two slices together. Enjoy your sandwich.

Writer uses strong verbs in steps.

Time-order words <u>organize</u> steps clearly.

Grammar

Nouns

A **noun** names a person, place, animal, or thing.

The **boy** and his **dog** played with a **ball** in the **yard.**

Boy names a person.
Dog names an animal.
Ball names a thing.
Yard names a place.

. . . .

Look at the sentence directions. Write the nouns in the sentences.

Let's Talk About
Working Together

Words to Read

you're
second
great
either
laugh
certainly
worst

Read the Words

You're invited to our second ball game of the year!

Come out and have a great time.

You will either laugh or cry, but you certainly will have fun.

We may have been the worst team last year, but this year will be our best ever!

Ronald Morgan Goes to Bat

Genre: Realistic Fiction
Realistic fiction has made-up characters that act like real people. Read about Ronald Morgan, who is an important member of his baseball team.

Ronald Morgan

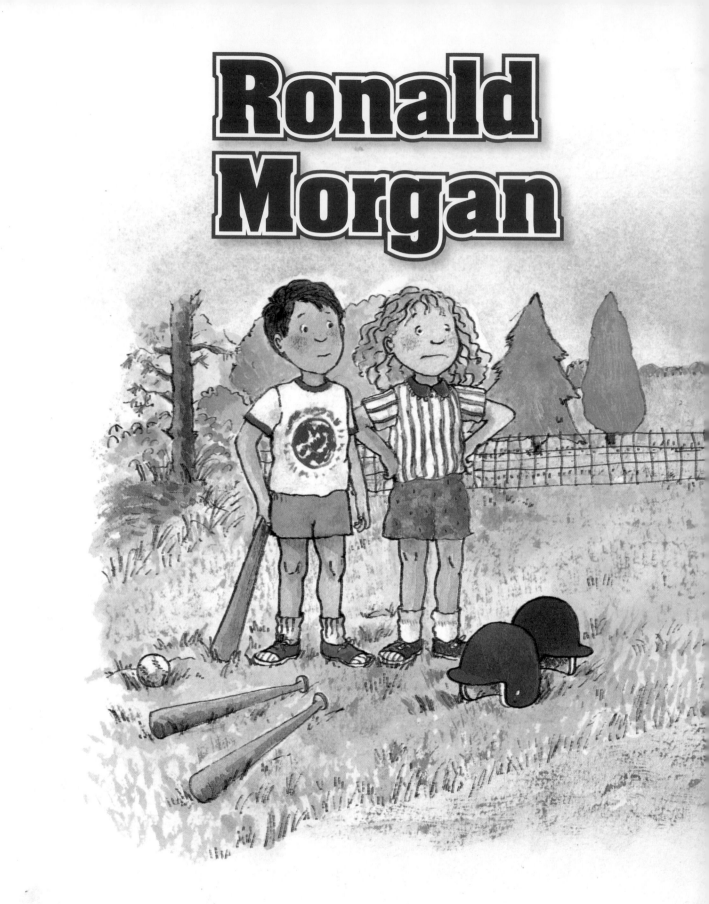

Goes to Bat

by Patricia Reilly Giff
illustrated by Susanna Natti

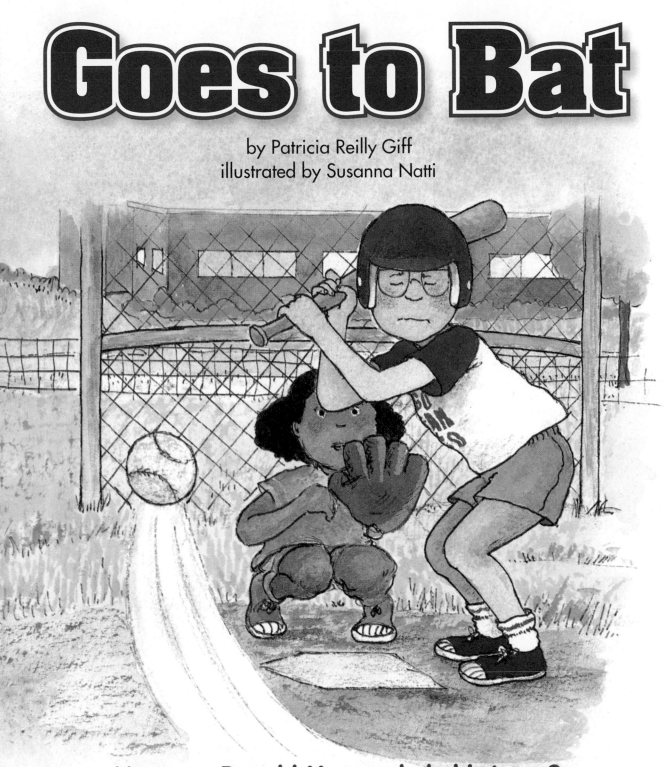

How can Ronald Morgan help his team?

Baseball started today. Mr. Spano
said everyone could play.

"Even me?" I asked.

And Tom said, "You're letting
Ronald Morgan play? He can't hit,
he can't catch. He can't do anything."

Mr. Spano looked at me.
"Everyone," he said.

"Yahoo!" I yelled. I pulled on my red and white shirt, the one that says GO TEAM GO, and ran outside to the field.

"Two things," Mr. Spano told us. "Try hard, and keep your eye on the ball."

Then it was time to practice. Michael was up first. He smacked the ball with the bat. The ball flew across the field.

"Good," said Mr. Spano.

"Great, Slugger!" I yelled. "We'll win every game."

It was my turn next. I put on the helmet
and stood at home plate.

"Ronald Morgan," said Rosemary. "You're
holding the wrong end of the bat."

Quickly I turned it around. I clutched it
close to the end.

Whoosh went the first ball.
Whoosh went the second one.
Wham went the third. It hit
me in the knee.

"Are you all right?" asked
Michael.

But I heard Tom say,
"I knew it. Ronald Morgan's
the worst."

At snack time, we told Miss Tyler about the team.

"I don't hit very well," I said.

And Rosemary said, "The ball hits him instead."

Everybody laughed, even me. I shook my head. "I hope it doesn't happen again."

Miss Tyler gave me some raisins. "You have to hit the ball before it hits you," she said.

We played every day. I tried hard, but the
ball came fast. I closed my eyes and swung.

"If only he could hit the ball once,"
Rosemary said.

And Billy shook his head.

I couldn't tell them I was afraid of the ball.
"Go, team, go," I whispered.

One day, the team sat on the grass.
We watched the third grade play. They
were big, they were strong, they were
good. Johnny hit a home run, and Joy
tagged a man out.

"We'll never hit like that," said Tom.

And Rosemary said, "We'll never catch like that either."

But I said, "Our team is the best."

Mr. Spano nodded. "That's the spirit, Ronald."

Mr. Spano told us, "Now we'll run the bases. Rosemary, you can go first."

Rosemary went fast. She raced for first base.

"Terrific, Speedy!" I yelled.

"Let me go next," I said. "I can do that, too."

But the field was muddy. My sneaker came off.

Jimmy said, "That kid's running bases the wrong way."

And Tom yelled, "Ronald Morgan. You're heading for third base."

The next day, we worked on catching.
I was out in left field. While I waited, I
found a stick, and started to scratch out
the mud. I wrote G for go. I wrote G for
great. Our team is the best, I thought.
Then I wrote H for hit. H for home run.
If only I could do that.

Just then I heard yelling. Someone had
hit the ball.

"Catch it, Ronald!" Tom shouted.

I put down the stick. I put up my mitt.
Too late. The ball sailed into the trees.

Mr. Spano took us for ice cream. "You
deserve it for trying," he said. "Our team is
really good."

I had a chocolate cone.

Michael's a slugger, I thought. And Rosemary can really run. But I'm still afraid of the ball.

On the way home, we saw some kids playing ball.

"Want to hit a few?" Michael asked.

I shook my head. "Maybe I won't play ball anymore."

Michael said, "We need you. You have spirit. You help the team feel good."

"But how can we win?" I asked. "I can't even hit the ball."

I saw my father and ran to catch up. "See you, Michael," I said.

My father asked, "How's the champ?"

"I'm the worst," I said.

"I was the worst, too," said my father. "But then. . . ."

"What?"

My father laughed. "I stopped closing my eyes when I swung."

"Maybe that's what I do."

"How about a little practice?" he asked.

We went into the yard. My father threw me some balls.

I missed the first one. . . . I missed the second. And then. . . . I opened my eyes and swung. *Crack* went the ball.

"Ouch!" went my father. "You hit me in the knee."

"Home run!" yelled my mother.

"Sorry," I said. "Hey, I did it!"

My father rubbed his knee. "You certainly did," he said.

I ran to pick up the ball. "See you later," I said.

My father smiled. "Where are you going?"

I grabbed the bat. "Some kids are playing ball. I think I'll hit a few."

I looked back. "And you know what else? I guess I'll stay on the team. I have spirit . . . and sometimes I can hit the ball. Mike was right. I think they need me."

Think and Share

Talk About It What would you say to Ronald Morgan to help him play baseball?

1. Use the pictures below to retell the story. Tell what might come after the last picture. Draw a picture. **Retell**

2. *Ronald Morgan Goes to Bat* is a realistic story. What would make it a fantasy? **Realism and Fantasy**

3. What do you know about playing sports? How did that help you as you read? **Prior Knowledge**

Look Back and Write Look back at page 209. What did Ronald's father say that was helpful? Why was it helpful? Use information from the selection to support your answer.

Meet the Author
Patricia Reilly Giff

Books are important to Patricia Reilly Giff. She says, "While the rest of the kids were playing hide and seek, I sat under the cherry tree reading." She also says, "I wanted to write—always."

Ms. Giff got married, had three children, and taught school. Then she decided to follow her dream. She began writing. Some books come from her experiences. Others come from stories students told her.

Read more books by Patricia Reilly Giff.

Spaceball

by Brod Bagert

illustrated by Tedd Arnold

Last night I had a funny dream—
My brain's a mysterious place.
I dreamed about some aliens
Who lived in outer space.

I watched them play a game
That seemed a lot like baseball.
They played with bats and floppy hats,
But the aliens called it Spaceball.

Jupiter was the pitcher's mound,
Saturn was third base,
And the little alien kid at bat
Had a serious look on his face.

"Full count, bottom of the ninth,"
I heard the announcer say.
"This batter's trying to hit the ball
Clean out of the Milky Way."

Then I saw the ball was planet Earth!
Oh, how could it possibly be?
If he hits *that* ball, it's the end of us all,
That means . . . THE END OF ME!

I heard a shout: "STRIKE THREE, YOU'RE OUT!"
And space was filled with cheers.
But the little alien batter's eyes
Filled up with alien tears.

My dreams are strange, but last night's dream
Was the strangest dream of all.
Earth was saved by an alien
Who couldn't hit the ball.

215

Write Now

Writing and Grammar

List

Prompt

In *Ronald Morgan Goes to Bat*, a boy plays on a baseball team. Think about a sports team you know.
Now write a list of facts about the team.

Student Model

Bullets separate facts on list.

Each sentence tells one fact.

Writer uses sentence conventions.

- Our baseball team is called the Ashland Astros.
- The Astros are in the Triple A League.
- We play at Legion Field on Saturdays.
- Hank Ori plays third base.
- Wally Ramos is catcher.

216

Grammar

Proper Nouns

Proper nouns are special names for people, places, animals, and things. They begin with capital letters.

Ronald took his dog **Tramp** to **Fisher Park.**

Days of the week, months of the year, and holidays also begin with capital letters.

• •

Look at the sentences in the list. Write the proper nouns from the sentences.

Let's Talk About
Working Together

Words to Read

toward
ago
word
whole
above
enough

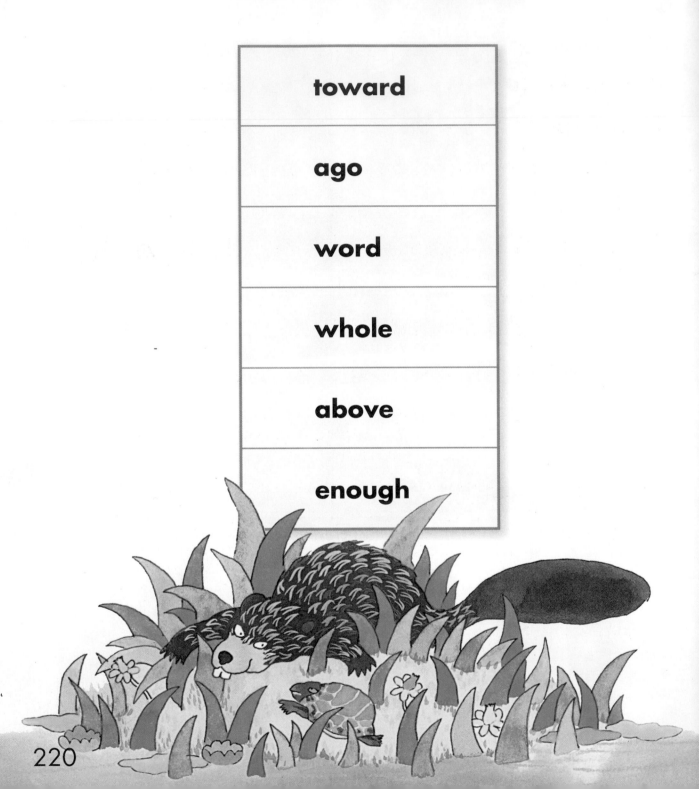

Read the Words

Beaver walked slowly toward the finish line. He had lost the race. Grandfather had told him long ago to always do his best. Beaver gave his word that he would. The whole forest had been cheering for him, but Turtle had won. Above all, Beaver had disappointed Grandfather. "Enough," Beaver told himself. "I will be a good sport and be happy for Turtle."

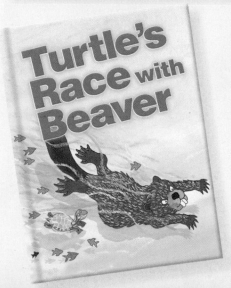

Genre: Folk Tale

A folk tale is a story that has been handed down from one generation to the next. Now you will read about Turtle and Beaver, who work out a problem by having a race.

Turtle's Race with Beaver

as told by Joseph Bruchac and James Bruchac
illustrated by Jose Aruego and Ariane Dewey

Why are Turtle and Beaver racing, and who will win?

Long ago, Turtle lived in a beautiful little pond.

She was very happy because this pond had everything a turtle needed. The water was just deep enough, there was plenty of food to eat, and there were lots of nice rocks just above the water for Turtle to sun herself on.

One day, as happens every year in the north, winter began to come to the land. As she had done year after year, Turtle swam to the bottom of the pond and buried herself in the thick mud.

While Turtle slept for the winter, another animal came walking along. It was Beaver, who had been looking for a new home.

"This will be perfect," said Beaver, "once I make some changes."

Soon he began doing one of the things beavers do so well. *Chomp! Chomp!* went Beaver as he took down one tree after another to build a big dam.

He worked hard for many days. And as
he did, the water got deeper and deeper.

After finishing his dam, Beaver made himself
a fine lodge of mud and sticks, then settled in
for the rest of the winter. He was very happy.

The moons came and went, and spring
returned once more to the land. The birds sang
and the ice melted away. Then Turtle woke up.
Crawling out from under the mud, she began to
swim toward the surface of the water. But she
had to swim higher, and higher, and higher,
and higher.

By the time Turtle made it to the surface, she
realized that the water was four times as deep
as before! Her pond didn't look the same at all.
All of the rocks she loved to sun herself on were
under water. On one side the pond stretched
as far as her eyes could see. On the other stood
a huge dam. Not too far from that was a big
round lodge.

Then Turtle heard a loud *Whack!* She turned to see where the sound had come from. A strange animal was swimming toward her. It was Beaver.

"Who are you?" asked Beaver. "What are you doing here?"

"I am Turtle," Turtle said. "This is my pond. I have lived here my whole life."

"*Your* pond!" said Beaver. "This is *my* pond! Look at my wonderful dam and my splendid lodge. This is a beaver's pond."

"Yes," Turtle said, "I can see that you've done lots of work. Couldn't we just share the pond? There's plenty of room."

"Ha!" Beaver laughed. "I will not share my pond with any little turtle. But I *will* challenge you to a race. Whoever wins can stay, whoever loses must go find a new home."

Turtle didn't really want to race. She could see that Beaver, with his big flat tail, was probably a much faster swimmer. But this pond was the only home she knew.

"I agree," Turtle said. "We will race."

It was decided that the race would take place the next morning at first light. The two would meet on one side of the pond and race to the other.

That night, Beaver told other animals about the race. Word began to spread throughout the forest.

Squirrel told Rabbit, Rabbit told Fox,
Fox told Wolf, Wolf told Deer, Deer told
Moose, Moose told Bear. Soon every
animal in the forest knew.

233

Before first light came to the land, all of the animals of the forest gathered around the pond. As they waited for Turtle and Beaver to arrive, many chose sides. Most of the smaller animals, such as Mouse, Chipmunk, and Rabbit, sided with Turtle. Most of the bigger animals, such as Wolf, Moose, and Bear, sided with Beaver.

As they waited, they began to sing:
TURTLE! BEAVER! TURTLE! BEAVER! TURTLE! BEAVER!

They sang even louder when Beaver came swimming over from his lodge and Turtle popped up from under the water.
TURTLE! BEAVER! TURTLE! BEAVER! TURTLE! BEAVER!

Turtle and Beaver took their
positions on the shore.

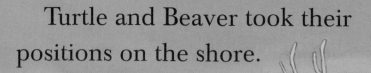

Bear lifted his big paw in the air.
"On your mark. . . get set. . . **GO!**"

SPLASH! went Beaver, leaping
off from the shore.

He was certain he would leave Turtle far behind. But Turtle had gotten an idea. Before Beaver hit the water, Turtle stretched out her long neck, opened her mouth, and bit into the end of Beaver's tail.

FLAP! FLAP! FLAP! went Beaver, swimming as fast as he could. But as fast as he went, Turtle was right behind, holding on as hard as she could.

The other animals kept cheering, but now some of the bigger animals were cheering for Turtle instead of Beaver.

TURTLE! BEAVER! TURTLE!
BEAVER! TURTLE! *TURTLE!*

Soon Beaver was halfway across the pond. Even though Turtle was still holding on, it looked as if Beaver would win for sure. Then Turtle bit a little harder into Beaver's tail.

FLAP! FLAP! FLAP! Beaver swam even faster. Turtle still held on. Now more of the animals were cheering for Turtle.

TURTLE! BEAVER! TURTLE!
TURTLE! TURTLE! TURTLE!

Now they were almost to the other side. Beaver seemed sure to win. But Turtle bit as hard as she could into Beaver's tail. *CRUNCH!*

"*YEEEE-OWWWW!*" yelled Beaver. He flipped his big flat tail up and out of the water. When his tail reached its highest point, Turtle let go.

"Weeee!" sang Turtle as she flew through the air right over Beaver's head.

KA-THUNK! Turtle landed on the far shore and crawled across the finish line. Turtle had won the race. All the animals cheered.

TURTLE! TURTLE! TURTLE!
TURTLE! TURTLE! TURTLE!

Turtle was very pleased. But she could see how sad Beaver was. "I would still be happy to share my pond," she said.

But Beaver was so embarrassed that he left without another word.

Over time Beaver's dam fell apart and the water got shallower and shallower. Turtle had back all her wonderful rocks to sun herself on.

As for Beaver, he did find a new home in a pond not too far away. In that pond, though, there also lived a turtle.

"Can I share your pond with you?" Beaver asked.

"Of course," that other turtle said.

And so the two of them lived there happily
through all the seasons to come.

Think and Share

Talk About It What lesson did Beaver learn? How would you explain the lesson to a friend?

1. The pictures below show what happened at the beginning of the story. Tell what happened in the middle and at the end. **Retell**

2. What was your favorite part of this story? What happened before and after that part? **Sequence**

3. Think about the race. How did it go? Summarize the part about the race. **Summarize**

TEST PRACTICE **Look Back and Write** Look back at pages 241 and 242. Did Beaver learn a lesson? How do you know? Use details from the story in your answer.

243

Meet the Authors

Joseph and James Bruchac

Read more books by Joseph or James Bruchac.

Joseph Bruchac retells Native American stories to share with children. Mr. Bruchac says the best stories teach important lessons, but they also must be fun. Mr. Bruchac and his son James often write together.

James Bruchac says, "Stories about animals are by far my favorites. Our animal brothers and sisters are always teaching us things." James Bruchac is a wilderness expert. He runs the Ndakinna Wilderness Project in Greenfield Center, New York, where he teaches classes on animal tracking, hiking, and the natural world.

Meet the Illustrators

Jose Aruego and Ariane Dewey

Jose Aruego and Ariane Dewey have created pictures for more than seventy books. Usually Mr. Aruego draws the lines and Ms. Dewey paints the colors.

Jose Aruego grew up in the Philippines. His family had all sorts of animals, including pigs, horses, dogs, cats, and chickens. "Most of the characters in my books are animals. No matter how I draw them, they look funny," he says.

Ariane Dewey likes paddling a kayak and watching birds. Her favorite animals are turtles, butterflies, penguins, and polar bears.

Read more books illustrated by these artists.

THE SECRET LIFE OF

PONDS

by Elizabeth Schleichert

from *Ranger Rick*

Have you ever explored a pond? If so, you know how awesome these small, still bodies of fresh water can be. Most ponds aren't all that deep or wide. But they're definitely worth hanging out at!

To really see all the creatures living in one, you may need to get up close.

That's what this girl is doing. She is even wearing a swim mask to see all the creatures darting, diving, squiggling, crawling, and swimming down here. Snails, snakes, beetles, fish, tadpoles, and spiders—who knows what she's discovering?

Sometimes you can catch hints of what's living at a pond as you get near one. Maybe the quacking of geese or ducks alerts you to water up ahead! You hear a loud *"plunk"* as a frog or turtle hits the water. Or you listen to the noisy *kon-ka-ree* of red-winged blackbirds.

Along the pond's edge, you may see some tracks: Looks as if deer have come down for a drink. Foxes, raccoons, and skunks have poked around for a meal too. *Shhh!* Look over there! It's a great blue heron, wading in the water. It's waiting for a tasty fish or frog to come close enough for easy snatching.

Who knows what *you* might find at a pond? For some possibilities, just turn the page.

What's Here?

The painting shows a pond in the Midwest or Northeast. You might not see all of these plants and animals in one pond. But you'll most likely see some.

1. fragrant water lily
2. green frog
3. sunfish
4. cattail
5. damselflies
6. water scorpion
7. orb snail
8. pickerel
9. leech
10. red-spotted newt
11. dragonfly
12. whirligig beetles
13. red-eared slider
14. shiner
15. giant water bug
16. bullhead

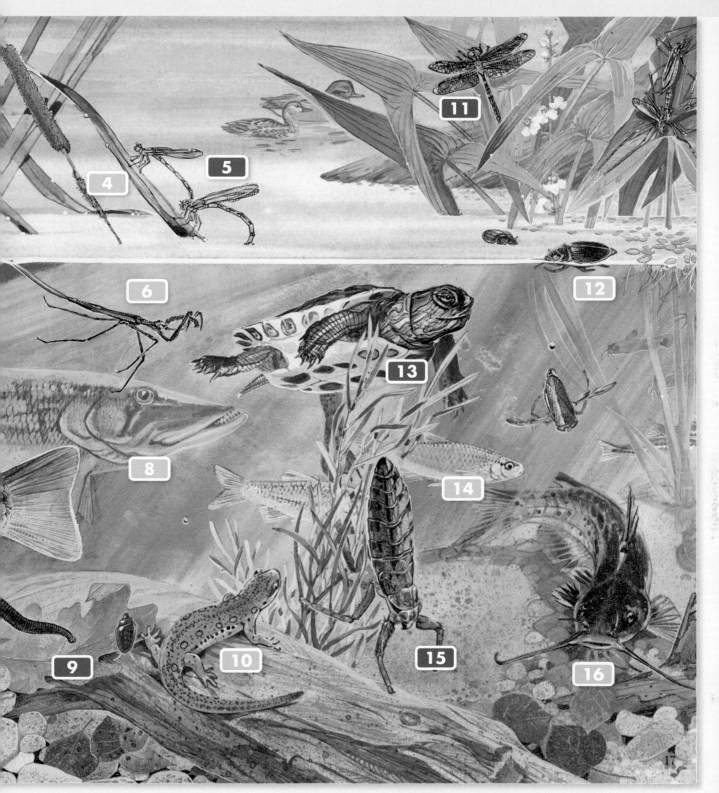

Plan

Prompt

In *Turtle's Race with Beaver*, Beaver learns about friendship.
Think about something special you could do for a friend.
Now write a plan that tells what you will do.

Writing Trait

Organize your plan in a way that makes sense.

Student Model

Writer identifies the plan.

Plan has clear details.

Plan is <u>organized</u> from first to last step.

I will make a bracelet for my friend Taylor. She likes bright colors, so I will use orange strings and yellow beads. I will wrap the bracelet in paper and put it on her desk. Then I will write a note to her. It will say that I am glad we are friends.

Grammar

Singular and Plural Nouns

A **singular noun** names one person, place, animal, or thing.

Turtle rested on the **rock.**

A noun that names more than one is called a **plural noun**.

Turtle could not find any **rocks.**

Add **-s** to most nouns to show more than one.

· ·

Write the singular nouns from the plan in one list. Write the plural nouns in another list.

Let's Talk About
Working Together

Words to Read

people
sign
bought
scared
probably
shall
pleasant

Read the Words

People waited for hours to get tickets for the big concert. One man made a sign asking for extra tickets! Some wise fans bought their tickets months ago. They were scared by all the talk that the concert would probably be sold out.

"I shall do my best," one singer said. "I think this will be a very pleasant concert."

Genre: Fairy Tale
A fairy tale usually takes place long ago and far away and has fantastic characters. Next you will read about four animals that become friends and travel to a faraway town.

The Bremen Town Musicians

retold as a play by Carol Pugliano-Martin
illustrated by Jon Goodell

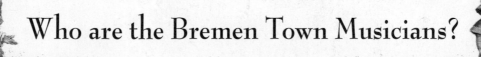

Who are the Bremen Town Musicians?

NARRATOR 1: Once there was a donkey. He worked hard for his owner for many years. Day after day he carried heavy bags of grain to the mill.

NARRATOR 2: But the donkey grew old. He could no longer work hard. One day he heard his owner talking about him. He said he was going to get rid of the donkey. The donkey was worried.

DONKEY: Oh, no! What will happen to me?
I must run away. I'll go to Bremen.
There I can be a fine musician.
(The donkey sings this song:)

Off I go to Bremen Town.
It's the place to be!
I will play my music there.
People will love me!
With a hee-haw here,
And a hee-haw there.
Here a hee, there a haw,
Everywhere a hee-haw.
Off I go to Bremen Town.
It's the place to be!

NARRATOR 1: So the donkey left that night. He had not gone far when he saw a dog lying on the ground.

NARRATOR 2: The dog looked weak. He also looked sad. The donkey knelt down to speak to the dog.

DONKEY: What is the matter, my friend?

DOG: Ah, me. Now that I am old and weak, I can no longer hunt. My owner wants to get rid of me. I got scared, so I ran away. Now I don't know what I will do.

DONKEY: You can come with me to Bremen. I am going to be a musician. Will you join me?

DOG: I'd love to! I can bark very pleasant tunes.

DOG AND DONKEY: Off we go to Bremen Town. It's the place to be! We will play our music there. We'll be filled with glee!

DONKEY: With a hee-haw here, and a hee-haw there. Here a hee, there a haw, everywhere a hee-haw.

DOG: With a bow-wow here and a bow-wow there. Here a bow, there a wow, everywhere a bow-wow.

DOG AND DONKEY: Off we go to Bremen Town. It's the place to be!

NARRATOR 1: So, the donkey and the dog set off for Bremen. Soon, they saw a cat sitting by the road.

NARRATOR 2: The cat had the saddest face the donkey and the dog had ever seen. They stopped to find out what was wrong.

DOG: Hello there. Why so glum?

CAT: Ho, hum. Now that I am old and my teeth are not sharp, I cannot catch mice. My owner wants to get rid of me. I don't know what I will do.

DONKEY: You'll come to Bremen with us, that's what! We are going to become musicians. Won't you join us?

CAT: Sure I will! I love to meow.

DONKEY, DOG, AND CAT:
Off we go to Bremen Town.
It's the place to be!
We will play our music there.
We're a gifted three!

DONKEY: With a hee-haw here,
and a hee-haw there.
Here a hee, there a haw,
everywhere a hee-haw.

DOG: With a bow-wow here,
and a bow-wow there.
Here a bow, there a wow,
everywhere a bow-wow.

CAT: With a meow-meow here,
and a meow-meow there.
Here a meow, there a meow,
everywhere a meow-meow.

ALL: Off we go to Bremen Town.
It's the place to be!

NARRATOR 1: The three musicians walked along some more. They came to a farmyard. There they heard a rooster crowing sadly.

ROOSTER: Cock-a-doodle-doo! Cock-a-doodle-doo!

DONKEY: My, you sound so sad. What is wrong?

ROOSTER: I used to crow to wake up the farmer each morning. But he just bought an alarm clock. Now he doesn't need my crowing so he wants to get rid of me. Now I'm a cock-a-doodle-*don't!* Oh, what will I do?

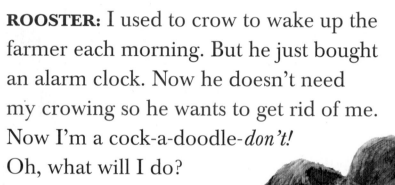

DOG: Come with us to Bremen. We're going to be musicians.

CAT: With your fine crowing, we'll make a wonderful group!

ROOSTER: I cock-a-doodle-*do* think that's a wonderful idea! Let's go!

DONKEY, DOG, CAT, AND ROOSTER:

Off we go to Bremen Town. It's the place to be!
We will play our music there. We're a sight to see!

DONKEY: With a hee-haw here, and a hee-haw there.
Here a hee, there a haw, everywhere a hee-haw.

DOG: With a bow-wow here, and a bow-wow there.
Here a bow, there a wow, everywhere a bow-wow.

CAT: With a meow-meow here, and a meow-meow
there. Here a meow, there a meow, everywhere a
meow-meow.

ROOSTER: With a cock-a-doodle here, and a cock-a-doodle there. Here a doodle, there a doodle, everywhere a cock-a-doodle.

ALL: Off we go to Bremen Town. It's the place to be!

NARRATOR 2: The four musicians walked until it got dark. Finally, they saw a sign that said Bremen Town. They danced with excitement, but they were also very tired. They wanted to rest.

NARRATOR 1: They saw light coming from a little house up the road. They walked up to the window, but none of the animals were tall enough to see inside. So, the dog stood on the donkey's back, the cat stood on the dog's back, and the rooster stood on the cat's back and peeked inside.

DOG: What do you see, rooster?

ROOSTER: I think there are three robbers in there! They are sitting at a table full of delicious-looking food!

CAT: Food? I'm starving! What shall we do? We must get them out of that house!

ROOSTER: I have a plan. Listen closely.

NARRATOR 2: The rooster whispered his plan to the others.

NARRATOR 1: All of a sudden, the four began singing. They made quite a noise. When the robbers heard the animals, they ran out of the house screaming!

NARRATOR 2: The four musicians went inside the house. There they ate and ate until they were full. Then, it was time for bed.

NARRATOR 1: The donkey slept in the soft grass in the yard. The dog slept behind the front door. The cat slept near the warmth of the fireplace. And the rooster slept high on a bookshelf.

NARRATOR 2: After a while, the robbers returned to finish eating their feast.

ROBBER 1: That noise was probably just the wind. Besides, I can't wait to eat the rest of that roast beef!

ROBBER 2: I can taste those mashed potatoes now!

ROBBER 3: I'll go first just to make sure it's safe.

NARRATOR 1: So the robber went inside. He was cold, so he went to the fireplace to warm himself. There he surprised the cat, who scratched his face.

NARRATOR 2: The robber ran to the front door. The dog was startled and bit his leg. The robber ran outside. He tripped over the donkey, who kicked him.

NARRATOR 1: All this noise woke the rooster up. He started screeching, "Cock-a-doodle-doo!" The robber ran back to his friends.

ROBBER 3: There are four horrible monsters in there! One scratched me with its long nails. Another bit me. Another kicked me. And the fourth one screamed, "Coming to get yooouuuuu!"

ROBBER 1: Four monsters! Let's get out of here!

NARRATOR 2: And the robbers ran off, never to be heard from again.

NARRATOR 1: But the four musicians stayed there. They sang every night in Bremen, where they became the famous Bremen Town Musicians!

Think and Share

Talk About It You have seen the Bremen Town Musicians perform. Tell about the show they put on for you.

1. Put the pictures below in order to tell the story of the Bremen Town Musicians. **Retell**

2. Why do you think the author wrote this story—to inform, entertain, or persuade? Explain.
Author's Purpose

3. This play has a beginning, middle, and end. The characters also have a problem. What is it, and how is it solved? **Story Structure**

Look Back and Write Why are the three robbers afraid of the animals? Look back at page 272. Use details from the story in your answer.

Meet the Author

Carol Pugliano-Martin

Carol Pugliano-Martin has written many plays for schoolchildren to perform. Some of her plays are about real Americans. Others tell about the heroes of American folk tales. Ms. Pugliano-Martin lives in White Plains, New York.

Here are two books by Carol Pugliano-Martin with plays you may want to perform.

Animals
Helping Animals

by Jacquelyn Siki

Did you know that some animals help one another? Sometimes they do this in unusual ways.

The sea animal that looks like a plant is called a *sea anemone*. The anemone will sting almost any fish that comes near it but not the clown fish. For some reason, the anemone does not hurt the clown fish. The clown fish can swim among the waving arms of the anemone and be safe from other fish that might try to hurt it.

Watch out! Has this crocodile found its lunch? No! This plover is a bird that helps keep the crocodile's mouth clean. It cleans the crocodile's teeth and mouth just like a dentist cleans your teeth.

What is this little cowbird doing? It's not getting a free ride. It's cleaning the insects off of the cow. The bird gets a meal. The cow gets clean.

This bird, called a *honey guide*, leads a *ratel*, or honey badger, to a beehive. The honey guide likes honey, and so does the badger. But the honey guide needs the badger's help to break open the hive. Then both animals can enjoy a treat!

These animals help each other too. When they are at a water hole together, baboons and impalas warn one another of danger. Baboons will even try to drive the danger away!

Like people, many animals help one another. They do this so that they can live together and survive.

279

Write Now

Writing and Grammar

Poster

Prompt

In *The Bremen Town Musicians,* a group of animals sings together. Think about a show at your school or in your community. Now write a poster that tells people about the show.

Student Model

First lines speak directly to readers.

> Attention men, women, and children! Don't miss the fun!

Writer **organizes** important information.

What: Hill Fun Fair

When: Tuesday, May 1, at 6 P.M.

Where: Hill School Gym

See amazing singers, dancers, jugglers, clowns, and much more.

Capital letters make word stand out.

Come and enjoy this FREE show!

Grammar

Plural Nouns That Change Spelling

A **plural noun** names more than one person, place, animal, or thing. Some nouns change spelling to name more than one.

one **mouse**	two **mice**
one **man**	two **men**
one **child**	two **children**

• •

Look at the poster. Write three plural nouns that change spelling. Write the singular form of each noun.

Let's Talk About
Working Together

282

Words to Read

| everybody |
| sorry |
| promise |
| minute |
| brought |
| behind |
| door |

284

Read the Words

It was the night before the big dinner. Everybody was coming—everybody but Sheep. Mr. Moose was sorry about that. But he made a promise to invite Sheep another time. Now Mr. Moose had to get busy. He didn't like to wait until the last minute to do anything. He brought in firewood from behind the door and began cooking. Soon the feast was ready.

A Turkey for Thanksgiving

Genre: Animal Fantasy
The animal characters in an animal fantasy act like people. Read about Mr. Moose and how he finds a turkey for Thanksgiving.

A Turkey for Thanksgiving

by Eve Bunting
illustrated by Diane deGroat

What will Mr. Moose do with a turkey for Thanksgiving?

It was Thanksgiving morning. Mr. Moose
helped Mrs. Moose set the Thanksgiving table.

"Sheep will sit here. He likes a chair that's
straight up and down," Mr. Moose said. "Rabbit
here. Porcupine here. Mr. and Mrs. Goat here."
He smiled at his wife. "Isn't it nice to have
friends to share Thanksgiving?"

Mrs. Moose set two paper pilgrims, one at each end of the table. She placed the paper turkey with its great fan of a tail between the candles, and stood back.

"They look good, my dear," Mr. Moose said.

Mrs. Moose sighed. "Yes. But I wish we had a real turkey. Everyone always has a turkey for Thanksgiving. Everyone but us."

Mr. Moose nuzzled Mrs. Moose's head. "Well, that won't do. I will go this minute and find you a turkey for Thanksgiving."

Mr. Moose put on his cap and went out.

Mist wandered through the bare trees. The cold made his nose water.

Rabbit poked his head from his rabbit hole. "Mr. Moose! Is it dinnertime?"

"Not quite yet. Mrs. Moose wants a turkey. I'm off to find one."

Rabbit joined him in three quick hops. "I'll come, too."

Moose's warm breath hung white in front of him. Snow crunched under his hooves and made little holes that Rabbit jumped over.

"I see the Goats," Rabbit said.

Mr. Goat raised his head and spat out the tin can he was chewing. "Is it dinnertime?" he called.

"Not till I find a turkey," Mr. Moose said.

"We saw one down by the river," Mrs. Goat told him, and Mr. Goat added, "A fat one."

The Goats leaped down from their perch.
"We'll show you."

Sheep was farther up the hillside, looking round
as a fur ball in his winter coat. "Is it dinnertime?"
he bellowed.

"First I have to find a turkey," Mr. Moose
bellowed back.

"There's a turkey nest on the riverbank,"
Sheep called. "Wait for me."

The earth smelled of ice and moss as they
crunched along. Above them a crow hung, black
as a puff of wood smoke.

Porcupine was hiding in the underbrush.

"It's you," he said and put his quills down.

"We're off to get a turkey for Mrs. Moose,"
Mr. Moose explained. "Do you want to come?"

"I'm slow," Porcupine said. "Pick me up on your
way back."

"Who'd want to pick you up?" Sheep asked, and
laughed his bleat of a laugh.

"I'll wait," Porcupine told Mr. Moose.

They saw Turkey's nest right away, and Turkey himself peering over the top of it.

"Turkey! Turkey!" Mr. Moose called in his sweetest voice.

"Aagh!" Turkey blundered from his nest and ran.

Mr. Moose lumbered after him. "Turkey! Don't run. We just want you for Thanksgiving dinner."

Turkey ran faster.

DO NOT DISTURB! (come back after Thanksgiving.)

NO Turkey here!

Mr. Moose saw the red and blue sheen of Turkey's neck. Turkey's tail brushed crumbs of snow behind him as he tried to fly.

"Too fat," Mr. Goat said.

Turkey's legs bent in the middle as he fell.

Mr. Moose put a booted hoof on his head and smiled his great, toothy smile. "I hope you don't have other plans for Thanksgiving, Turkey."

He helped Turkey up. "My wife won't mind that you're too fat," he said. "Let's go. It's getting close to dinnertime."

They marched Turkey in front. "I'm sorry about this, for I can see you don't want to come," Mr. Moose said. "But I must insist. A promise is a promise."

There was a wreath of dried fruit on the Mooses'
door. Inside, the house was filled with Thanksgiving
smells. Mr. Moose hid Turkey behind him.

"Look who I brought, Mrs. Moose," he said.
"Sheep, the Goats, Rabbit, and Porcupine. And
ta-da!" He pushed Turkey around in front of him.
"For you. A turkey for Thanksgiving!"

Mrs. Moose clapped her hooves. "I'm *so* happy
to have you, Turkey. Thank you, Mr. Moose. Now
everything's perfect."

"Shall we sit?" Sheep asked, heading for the straight-up-and-down chair.

"Let's." Mrs. Moose pointed. "Rabbit here. Porcupine here. Mr. and Mrs. Goat here, and look! I brought a chair from the other room in hopes of Turkey."

"A . . . a *chair*?" Turkey stammered.

"Right next to me," Mrs. Moose said. "Light the candles, Mr. Moose."

There were bowls of acorns and alfalfa sprouts, dried since summer. There was willow bark and cured grasses and wild parsley. There were pressed leaves, thin and pale as new ice on a pond.

"I hope you find something here to your liking, Mr. Turkey," Mrs. Moose said. "I wasn't sure of your taste."

"You are so kind to worry about my taste," Turkey said. "I thought you'd be worrying about *how* I'd taste."

"Heavens, no!" Mr. Moose smiled his big-toothed smile and filled everyone's cup with cold spring water. "It's so nice to have friends around the table at Thanksgiving."

Turkey's wattles wobbled. "It's even nicer to be AT your table and not ON it," he said. "Happy Thanksgiving, everybody."

"Happy Thanksgiving, Turkey."

Think and Share

Talk About It Pretend you are Turkey. Tell why you are afraid to come to dinner.

1. The pictures below show the beginning, middle, and end of the story. Retell the story. Fill in the missing parts. **Retell**

2. What conclusion did Turkey draw? Why would he think that? **Draw Conclusions**

3. Read page 295 again. What picture do you have in your mind as you read that page? **Visualize**

Look Back and Write Look back at page 300. Make a list of the foods Mrs. Moose served her guests. How do you think everyone enjoyed the dinner? What makes you think so?

Meet the Author
Eve Bunting

Read other books by Eve Bunting.

Eve Bunting does not eat turkey. She always thinks "poor turkey" when she sees a bird being put into the oven. That feeling is where she got the idea for *A Turkey for Thanksgiving,* one of her favorite books.

Ms. Bunting grew up in Ireland. There they do not celebrate a holiday like Thanksgiving.

Ms. Bunting loves to write. She has written over two hundred books for children. She has written about giants and ogres and creatures with scales and fins. She has written about sharks and whales and giant squid. She has written about children growing up and men growing old. Writing an animal fantasy like *A Turkey for Thanksgiving* is her "fun and relaxing time."

304

Meet the Illustrator
Diane deGroat

Diane deGroat has "a large picture file with photos of everything in the whole wide world." She used that file to help her draw the animals for *A Turkey for Thanksgiving*.

Read two more books illustrated by Diane deGroat.

She likes changing pictures of real animals into the characters in a story. "It's fun to choose what clothes they wear and what kind of expressions they should have." The turkeys were the hardest to draw. "They are not the most attractive birds, if you know what I mean."

Thanksgiving USA

After reading *A Turkey for Thanksgiving*, Nadia wants to learn more about the Thanksgiving holiday. With her parents' permission, Nadia searches the Web. She finds a Web site with many links.

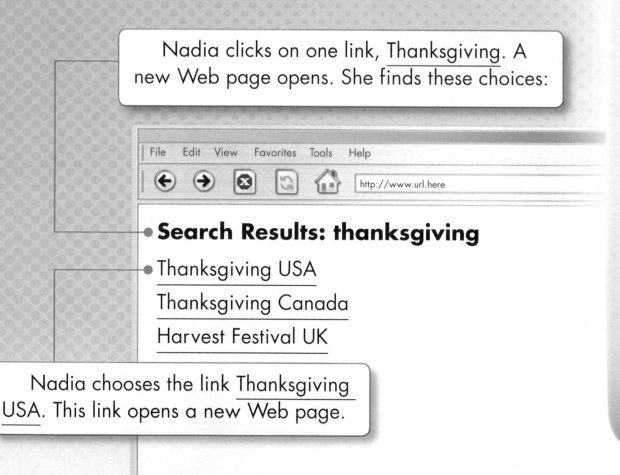

Nadia clicks on one link, Thanksgiving. A new Web page opens. She finds these choices:

File   Edit   View   Favorites   Tools   Help

http://www.url.here

- **Search Results: thanksgiving**

- Thanksgiving USA

  Thanksgiving Canada

  Harvest Festival UK

Nadia chooses the link Thanksgiving USA. This link opens a new Web page.

For more practice

Take It to the Net

PearsonSuccessNet.com

Thanksgiving USA

In 1620 a ship, the Mayflower, sailed across the Atlantic Ocean. It was headed to America. About one hundred people were on this ship. The Pilgrims, as they were called, traveled to what is now Massachusetts. Their first winter was hard. They had come too late to plant and grow food. Without fresh food, half of the Pilgrims died.

The following spring, the Iroquois Indians showed the Pilgrims how to grow corn and other plants. The Indians showed the Pilgrims how to hunt and fish. By the fall of 1621, the Pilgrims had grown a lot of food. They had much to be thankful for. They planned a huge day for giving thanks. They invited the Indian chief and 90 Indians. The Indians brought deer to roast and other foods. The Indians had taught the Pilgrims different ways to cook corn and squash. The Indians even brought popcorn to this first Thanksgiving.

Nadia uses the scroll bar on the right-hand side of the Web page to find out more about Thanksgiving.

File   Edit   View   Favorites   Tools   Help

http://www.url.here

Many years later, the U.S. Congress asked that one day every year be set aside for the whole country to celebrate and give thanks. George Washington chose the date November 26 as Thanksgiving Day. Then in 1863, Abraham Lincoln asked all Americans to set aside the last Thursday in November as a day of thanksgiving.

Today, Thanksgiving falls on a different date every year, but it is always on the fourth Thursday of November.

Write Now

Writing and Grammar

Invitation

Prompt
In *A Turkey for Thanksgiving*, friends celebrate Thanksgiving.
Think about celebrating a family member's birthday.
Now write an invitation to the birthday party.

Student Model

Event is stated at beginning.

Come to Grandpa's 70th Birthday Party!

Form helps writer <u>focus</u> on important <u>ideas</u>.

<u>Date:</u> Sunday, July 8

<u>Time:</u> 2:00 P.M.

<u>Place:</u> Veterans' Hall

All information is about the party.

<u>What to Bring:</u> a favorite memory of Grandpa to share with everyone. Please reply by July 1.

Writer's Checklist

 Focus Does all the informtion tell about a party?

 Organization Is the information written in the from of an invitation?

 Support Does the invitation tell readers when and where?

 Conventions Are apostrophes used correctly?

 Grammar

Possessive Nouns

A noun that shows who or what owns something is a **possessive noun.** To show ownership, add an **apostrophe (')** and **-s** when the noun is singular.

the **goat's** pen (one goat)

Add just an **apostrophe** when the noun is plural.

the **goats'** pen (more than one goat)

• •

Write the possessive nouns in the invitation. Which is singular? How do you know?

311

Wrap-Up

Working Together Poster

connect to

WRITING

Think about all the stories you read in this unit. What lessons did you learn from them? Work with a group. Make a list of rules for working together in school. Talk about what you learned from the stories as you make your list.

Rules for Working Together

1.
2.
3.
4.
5.

How can we work together?

Go Along, Get Along Sock Puppets

connect to

DRAMA

Choose two characters from different stories in Unit 2. Make a sock puppet for each one. Have the two puppets talk to each other. They should tell about what happened to them and what they learned about working together with others.

Team Member Award

connect to
SOCIAL
STUDIES

Ronald Morgan was not a great hitter, but he was an important part of his team. Think about how you add something important to a group. Make an award for yourself. The award should show and tell about how you help the group as you work together.

Tony
the Reading helper
I help other kids read
hard books.

Creative Ideas

What does it mean to be creative?

Pearl and Wagner: Two Good Friends

Friends share a creative idea.

ANIMAL FANTASY

connect to SCIENCE

Dear Juno

A boy finds a creative way to write to his grandmother.

REALISTIC FICTION

connect to SOCIAL STUDIES

Anansi Goes Fishing

Anansi's creative idea backfires.

FOLK TALE

connect to SCIENCE

Rosa and Blanca

Sisters surprise each other with a creative idea.

REALISTIC FICTION

connect to SOCIAL STUDIES

A Weed Is a Flower

An important scientist had a creative mind.

BIOGRAPHY

connect to SCIENCE

315

Let's Talk About
Creative Ideas

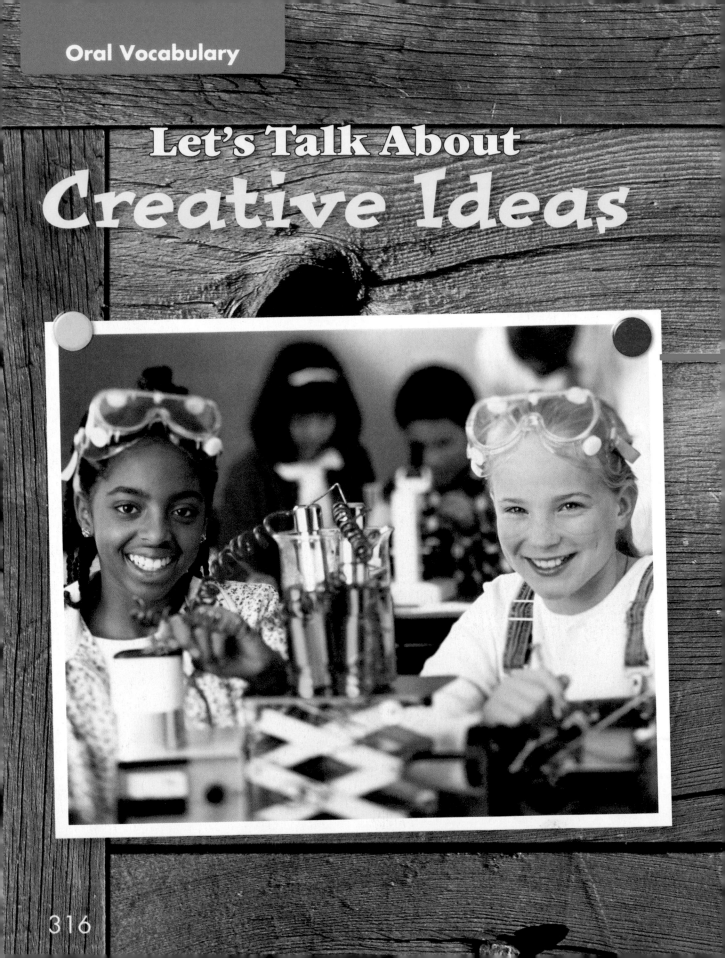

Words to Read

shoe

science

village

guess

won

pretty

watch

Read the Words

"Pearl?" Wagner asked. "Did you ever find your shoe?"

"Yes," Pearl said. "I lost it at the science fair when you opened the ant village."

"I guess setting the ants free was a bad idea. I just wanted to win a prize."

"Well, nobody won because ants were everywhere," said Pearl. "It wasn't a pretty sight."

"I guess it's better to watch ants from the outside in," Wagner said.

"I guess it is," Pearl replied.

Genre: Animal Fantasy
In an animal fantasy, the animal characters act like humans. Next, you will read about Pearl and Wagner at the science fair.

Pearl and Wagner

Two Good Friends

by Kate McMullan · illustrated by R.W. Alley

What creative idea will help Pearl and Wagner remain good friends?

Plants love music

See the effect of music on planted in the pot marigolds.

DANGER KEEP AWAY

321

The Robot

Everyone in Ms. Star's class was talking about the Science Fair.

"I am going to make a robot," said Pearl.

"I am going to win a prize," said Wagner.

Pearl got to work. She taped up the flaps
of a great big box. She cut a hole in the top.
Then she cut a hole in the lid of a shoe box.
She glued the shoe box lid to the top of the
great big box. Wagner held the boxes together
while the glue dried.

"Maybe I will make a walkie-talkie," he said.

Pearl punched a hole in one end of the shoe box. She stuck string through the hole. She tied the string in a knot.

"Maybe I will make a brain out of clay," said Wagner.

"Cool," said Pearl.

She drew eyes and a nose on the shoe box. Wagner looked at the shoe box.

"The eyes are too small," he said.

Pearl made the eyes bigger.

"Maybe I will make a rocket," said Wagner. "*Vrooom!* Blast off!"

Pearl put the shoe box onto the lid.

"There!" she said. "Finished!"
Pearl pulled the string.
The robot's mouth opened.
She threw in a wad of paper.
Then she let go of the string.
The robot's mouth shut.
    "Wow!" said Wagner.
"A trash-eating robot!"

"Let's see what everyone has made," said Ms. Star.

"Uh-oh," said Wagner. He had not made anything yet.

Lulu raised her hand. "I made a walkie-talkie," she said.

"I was going to do that!" said Wagner.

"I made paper airplanes," said Bud. "This chart shows how far they flew."

Wagner slapped his head. "Why didn't *I* think of that?"

Henry showed how to get electricity from a potato.

"Henry is a brain," said Pearl.

"Pearl?" Wagner said. "Remember how I held the boxes together while the glue dried?"

"I remember," said Pearl.

"Remember how I told you to give the robot bigger eyes?" asked Wagner.

Pearl nodded. "I remember."

"Your turn, Pearl," said Ms. Star.

"I made a trash-eating robot," said Pearl. She looked at Wagner. He was slumped down in his seat.

"Wagner and I made it together," said Pearl. Wagner sat right up again.

Pearl pulled the robot's string. She pulled too hard. The robot's head fell off.

"Uh-oh," said Wagner.

"I guess you two friends have more work to do," said Ms. Star.

"I guess so," said Pearl. "But I don't mind, because Wagner and I will do all of the work together."

"Uh-oh," said Wagner.

The Science Fair

On Science Fair Day, Pearl and Wagner were still working on their robot. Pearl stretched rubber bands. She held them tight. Wagner stapled them onto the shoe box and the lid.

"That should do it," he said.

Pearl and Wagner hurried to the gym with their robot. They passed a boy with an ant village. They passed a girl playing music for plants. They passed Henry. He had his electric potato hooked up to a tiny Ferris wheel.

Pearl and Wagner set
up their robot.

A judge came over.

"Watch this," said
Pearl. Pearl pulled
the robot's string. Nothing happened.
She pulled harder. The robot's mouth popped
open. The rubber bands flew everywhere.

"Yikes!" said the judge.

"Oh, no!" said Wagner. "There goes our prize!"

"We are not quite ready," Pearl told the judge.

"I will come back in five minutes,"
said the judge.

"I have more rubber bands in my desk," said Pearl. She raced off to get them.

Wagner tapped his foot. He bit his nails. Pearl was taking forever! The judge would be back any second. He had to *do* something.

Wagner looked around. No one was watching him. He pulled the tape off the big box. He opened the back of the robot and slipped inside.

The judge came back. She did not see
Pearl and Wagner. She started to leave.
"Wait!" said the robot.
"Oh, my stars!" said the judge.
"A talking robot!"

Just then Pearl came back.

"You have a nice smile," the robot was telling the judge. "And such pretty eyes."

"Do you think so?" said the judge.

Pearl could not believe her ears.

"Your robot is so smart!" said the judge. "How does it work?"

"Uh . . ." said Pearl. "It is hard to explain."

The judge opened the robot's mouth. She looked inside.

"Hi there!" said Wagner.

"Uh-oh," said Pearl.

335

The judge gave out the prizes. The girl who played music for plants won first prize. Henry and his electric potato won second prize. The trash-eating robot did not win any prize at all.

"I was only trying to help," Wagner told Pearl.
"I know," said Pearl. "You are a good friend,
Wagner. And you were a pretty good robot too."

Think and Share

Talk About It Do you think this story has a sad or happy ending? Why do you think so?

1. Use the pictures below to retell the story. Then draw a picture of what happens after the story is over.
Retell

2. Was the author trying to make you laugh, explain something, or give you information? Explain what makes you think that. **Author's Purpose**

3. What problem do Pearl and Wagner have in the middle of the story? How is it solved at the end?
Story Structure

Look Back and Write Look back at pages 333–335. Why do you think the talking robot didn't win a prize? Use details from the selection.

About the Author and the Illustrator
Kate McMullan

Kate McMullan loves to read. When asked what she wanted to be when she grew up, she always said, "A reader." When she decided to try writing, she moved to New York City.

Read more books by Kate McMullan.

R. W. Alley

R. W. Alley has illustrated many books for children. He says Kate McMullan had been thinking of a dog and a cat as Pearl and Wagner. But when she saw his mouse and his rabbit, she approved.

Robots at home

from *Robots* by Clive Gifford

Robots are coming home. The latest robots are doing useful chores around the house. Home robots need to know their way around a house and be able to communicate with their owners.

Ready for breakfast?

Robots cannot cook your meals yet, but they can carry them to you. Home robots often hold a map of the house in their memory. They also need sensors to know when household objects are in their way.

Beware of the dog.

This robot guard dog patrols the house, checking that everything is safe. If it notices anything wrong, it can take pictures and send them to the owner's cell phone.

Home playmates

PaPeRos wander around the house looking for people to talk to. They can recognize 650 different words and phrases and can speak up to 3,000 words. They can even dance!

341

Write Now

Plan

Prompt

Pearl and Wagner tells about two friends who make a robot. Think about a robot you would make. Now write a plan that tells what you would do.

Writing Trait

Use a serious **voice,** or tone, in a plan.

Student Model

Each sentence tells an action.

Ideas are in an order that makes sense.

Voice of plan is serious.

I decide what my robot will do.

I research the best way to make my robot.

I gather the materials I need.

I build my robot.

I test it to see if it works.

Verbs

A word that shows action is a **verb.**

Pearl and Wagner **make** a robot.

The word **make** is a verb. It tells what Pearl and Wagner do.

• •

A robot could <u>walk</u>. Name three other verbs that tell actions a robot could do.

Let's Talk About
Creative Ideas

Words to Read

picture
school
answer
faraway
parents
wash
company

346

Read the Words

Dear Grandma,

    Thank you for your letter and the picture. I took them to school. I had to answer many questions from my friends. I told them that you lived in a faraway place called Korea. I told them that my parents will take me there soon.

    I must go now and wash my hands. We are having company for dinner.

          Love,
          Juno

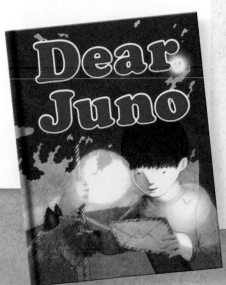

Genre: Realistic Fiction

Realistic fiction has characters, a setting, and a plot that could be real. This next story is about Juno, a boy who finds a creative way to write to his grandmother.

Dear Juno

by Soyung Pak

illustrated by Susan Kathleen Hartung

Who has written a letter to Juno?

Juno watched as the red and white blinking lights soared across the night sky like shooting stars, and waited as they disappeared into faraway places. Juno wondered where they came from. He wondered where they were going. And he wondered if any of the planes came from a little town near Seoul where his grandmother lived, and where she ate persimmons every evening before bed.

Juno looked at the letter that came that day. It was long and white and smudged. He saw the red and blue marks on the edges and knew the letter came from far away. His name and address were neatly printed on the front, so he knew the letter was for him. But best of all, the special stamp on the corner told Juno that the letter was from his grandmother.

 Through the window Juno could see his
parents. He saw bubbles growing in the sink. He
saw dirty dishes waiting to be washed. He knew
he would have to wait for the cleaning to be done
before his parents could read the letter to him.

"Maybe I can read the inside, too," Juno said
to his dog, Sam. Sam wagged his tail. Very
carefully, Juno opened the envelope. Inside, he
found a letter folded into a neat, small square.

He unfolded it. Tucked inside were a picture
and a dried flower.

Juno looked at the letters and words he couldn't understand. He pulled out the photograph. It was a picture of his grandmother holding a cat. He pulled out the red and yellow flower. It felt light and gentle like a dried leaf. Juno smiled. "C'mon, Sam," Juno said. "Let's find Mom and Dad."

355

"Grandma has a new cat," Juno said as he handed the letter to his mother. "And she's growing red and yellow flowers in her garden."

"How do you know she has a new cat?" Juno's father asked.

"She wouldn't send me a picture of a strange cat," said Juno.

"I guess not," said Juno's father.

"How do you know the flower is from her garden?" asked Juno's mother.

"She wouldn't send me a flower from someone else's garden," Juno answered.

"No, she wouldn't," said Juno's mother.

Then Juno's mother read him the letter.

356

Dear Juno,

How are you? I have a new cat to keep me company. I named him Juno after you. He can't help me weed, but the rabbits no longer come to eat my flowers.

Grandma

"Just like you read it yourself," Juno's father said.

"I did read it," Juno said.

"Yes, you did," said his mother.

At school, Juno showed his class his grandmother's picture and dried flower. His teacher even pinned the letter to the board. All day long, Juno kept peeking at the flower from his grandmother's garden. He didn't have a garden that grew flowers, but he had a swinging tree.

Juno looked at the letter pinned to the board. Did his grandmother like getting letters too? Yes, Juno thought. She likes getting letters just like I do. So Juno decided to write one.

After school, Juno ran to his backyard. He picked a leaf from the swinging tree—the biggest leaf he could find.

Juno found his mother, who was sitting at her desk. He showed her the leaf. "I'm going to write a letter," he told her.

"I'm sure it will be a very nice letter," she answered, and gave him a big yellow envelope.

"Yes it will," Juno said, and then he began to draw.

First, he drew a picture of his mom and dad standing outside the house. Second, he drew a picture of Sam playing underneath his big swinging tree. Then very carefully, Juno drew a picture of himself standing under an airplane in a starry, nighttime sky. After he was finished, he placed everything in the envelope.

"Here's my letter," Juno announced proudly. "You can read it if you want."

Juno's father looked in the envelope.

He pulled out the leaf. "Only a big swinging
tree could grow a leaf this big," he said.

Juno's mother pulled out one of the drawings.
"What a fine picture," she said. "It takes a good
artist to say so much with a drawing."

Juno's father patted Juno on the head. "It's
just like a real letter," he said.

"It is a real letter," Juno said.

"It certainly is," said his mother. Then they
mailed the envelope and waited.

One day a big envelope came. It was from Juno's grandmother. This time, Juno didn't wait at all. He opened the envelope right away.

Inside, Juno found a box of colored pencils. He knew she wanted another letter.

Next, he pulled out a picture of his grandmother. He noticed she was sitting with a cat and two kittens. He thought for a moment and laughed. Now his grandmother would have to find a new name for her cat—in Korea, Juno was a boy's name, not a girl's.

Then he pulled out a small toy plane.

Juno smiled. His grandmother was coming to visit.

"Maybe she'll bring her cat when she comes to visit," Juno said to Sam as he climbed into bed. "Maybe you two will be friends."

Soon Juno was fast asleep.
And when he dreamed that
night, he dreamed about a
faraway place, a village just
outside Seoul, where his
grandmother, whose gray hair
sat on top of her head like
a powdered doughnut, was
sipping her morning tea.

The cool air feels crisp
against her cheek. Crisp
enough to crackle, he dreams,
like the golden leaves which
cover the persimmon garden.

Think and Share

Talk About It Plan a letter without words to someone. Put three things in the letter, but only one can be a picture. What will you send?

1. Look at the pictures below. They are mixed up. Tell the correct order to retell the story. **Retell**

2. Can you tell how Juno feels about his grandmother? What makes you think that? **Draw Conclusions**

3. What picture did you have in your mind each time Juno spoke of his grandmother? How did visualizing help you? **Visualize**

Look Back and Write Reread page 362. What did a small toy airplane mean to Juno? Use information from the story in your answer.

About the Author and the Illustrator

Soyung Pak

Soyung Pak was born in South Korea. When she was two years old, she moved to New Jersey. When a plane flew overhead, her family waved. They pretended Grandmother was on the plane, coming from Korea.

Read more books by Soyung Pak.

Susan Kathleen Hartung

Susan Hartung has always loved to draw. As a child, she sometimes got in trouble for her pictures. Finally she learned to do her drawings on paper!

SAYING IT WITHOUT WORDS
Signs and Symbols

by Arnulf K. Esterer and Louise A. Esterer

Have you seen signs like these:

- the arrow on a one-way street?
- the EXIT sign over doors in the school auditorium?
- the big letter M over a hamburger shop downtown?

These are a few examples of signs. You have seen many more all around you. A sign tells you exactly what to do or what is there.

ONE WAY

EXIT

Have you seen:

- a happy face on your milk mug?
- the flag of our country waving from a building?
- a drawing of the atom in advertising?

These are a few examples of symbols. They tell about something. Symbols are like pictures of ideas.

Look around. See how many signs and symbols you can find. We use them every day. See how much they help you to know what to do or where to go.

Good signs and symbols tell you something—and fast! They tell you even if you can't read, or even if it's in a foreign language.

One look is all you usually need. One look tells it.

Write Now

Writing and Grammar

List

Prompt

In *Dear Juno*, a boy writes to his grandmother.
Think about what you could write about in a letter.
Now write a list of these things.

Student Model

Each item <u>focuses</u> on one <u>idea</u>.

Details make items interesting.

Related ideas are listed together.

<u>News I Can Use in My Letter</u>

Tracy and I go to the zoo.

We feed a camel!

We watch polar bears swim.

Amy eats a bug!

Spot digs up a bone.

Mom and Dad take us to a

movie. We like it.

Grammar

Verbs with Singular and Plural Nouns

Add **-s** to a verb to tell what one person, animal, or thing does. Do not add **-s** to a verb that tells what two or more people, animals, or things do.

> Grandma **mails** a letter to Juno.
> The pictures **tell** a story.

• •

Look at the list. Write the verbs from the sentences. Circle the verbs that tell what one person, animal, or thing does.

Let's Talk About
Creative Ideas

Words to Read

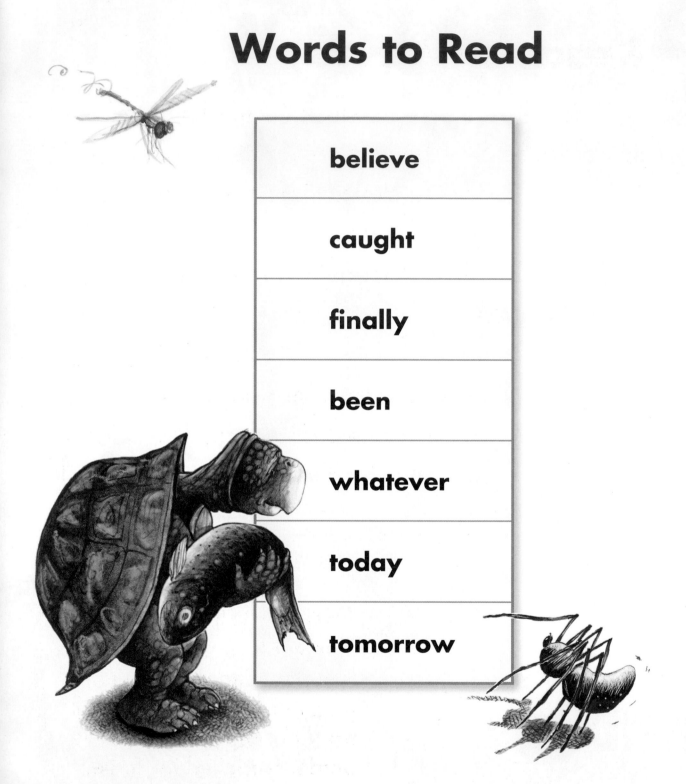

believe
caught
finally
been
whatever
today
tomorrow

Read the Words

"I do believe you are stuck," said the spider to the fly who was caught in his web.

"Finally," said the clever fly to the spider. "I've been waiting for you."

"Whatever do you mean?" the spider asked, surprised.

"You invited me over today," the fly said. "Why would you set a trap for your friend?"

The confused spider helped free the fly.

As the fly flew off, he called, "Better clever today than lunch tomorrow!"

Genre: Folk Tale

A folk tale is a story that has been handed down over many years. Now, you will read about how Anansi the Spider is tricked by Turtle.

Anansi
Goes Fishing

retold by Eric A. Kimmel
illustrated by Janet Stevens

What will Anansi catch when he goes fishing?

One fine afternoon Anansi the Spider was
walking by the river when he saw his friend
Turtle coming toward him carrying a large fish.
Anansi loved to eat fish, though he was much too
lazy to catch them himself.

"Where did you get that fish?"
he asked Turtle.

"I caught it today when I went fishing,"
Turtle replied.

"I want to learn to catch fish too," Anansi
said. "Will you teach me?"

"Certainly!" said Turtle. "Meet me by the river
tomorrow. We will go fishing together. Two can
do twice the work of one."

But Anansi did not intend to do any work at all. "Turtle is slow and stupid," he said to himself. "I will trick him into doing all the work. Then I will take the fish for myself." But Turtle was not as stupid as Anansi thought.

Early the next morning, Turtle arrived. "Are you ready to get started, Anansi?" he asked.

"Yes!" Anansi said. "I have been waiting a long time. I want to learn to catch fish as well as you do."

"First we make a net," said Turtle. "Netmaking is hard work. When I do it myself, I work and get tired. But since there are two of us, we can share the task. One of us can work while the other gets tired."

"I don't want to get tired," Anansi said. "I'll make the net. You can get tired."

"All right," said Turtle. He showed Anansi how to weave a net. Then he lay down on the riverbank.

"This is hard work," Anansi said.

"I know," said Turtle, yawning. "I'm getting very tired."

Anansi worked all day weaving the net. The harder he worked, the more tired Turtle grew. Turtle yawned and stretched, and finally he went to sleep. After many hours the net was done.

"Wake up, Turtle," Anansi said. "The net is finished."

Turtle rubbed his eyes. "This net is strong and light. You are a fine netmaker, Anansi. I know you worked hard because I am very tired. I am so tired, I have to go home and sleep. Meet me here tomorrow. We will catch fish then."

The next morning Turtle met Anansi by the river again.

"Today we are going to set the net in the river," Turtle said. "That is hard work. Yesterday you worked while I got tired, so today I'll work while you get tired."

"No, no!" said Anansi. "I would rather work than get tired."

"All right," said Turtle. So while Anansi worked hard all day setting the net in the river, Turtle lay on the riverbank, getting so tired he finally fell asleep.

"Wake up, Turtle," Anansi said, hours later. "The net is set. I'm ready to start catching fish."

Turtle yawned. "I'm too tired to do any more today, Anansi. Meet me here tomorrow morning. We'll catch fish then."

Turtle met Anansi on the riverbank the next morning.

"I can hardly wait to catch fish," Anansi said.

"That's good," Turtle replied. "Catching fish is hard work. You worked hard these past two days, Anansi. I think I should work today and let you get tired."

"Oh, no!" said Anansi. "I want to catch fish. I don't want to get tired."

"All right," said Turtle. "Whatever you wish."

Anansi worked hard all day pulling the net out of the river while Turtle lay back, getting very, very tired.

How pleased Anansi was to find a large fish caught in the net!

"What do we do now?" he asked Turtle.

Turtle yawned. "Now we cook the fish. Cooking is hard work. I think I should cook while you get tired."

"No!" cried Anansi. He did not want to share any bit of the fish. "I will cook. You get tired."

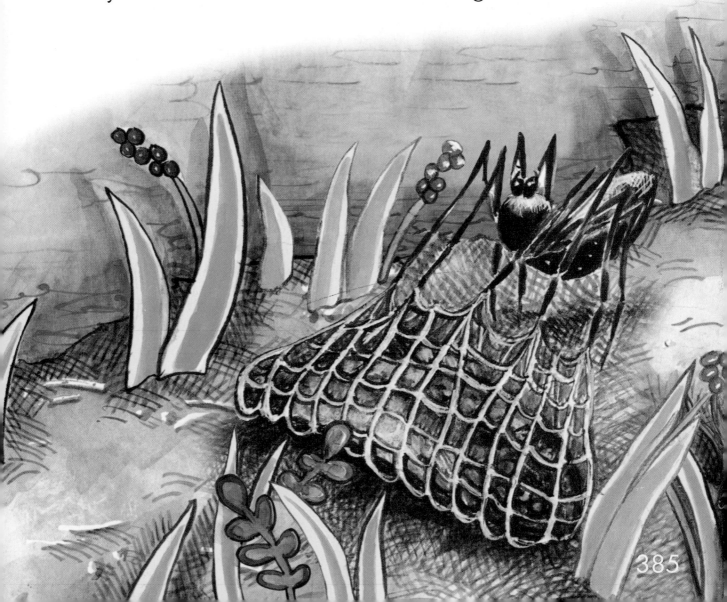

While Turtle watched, Anansi built a fire and cooked the fish from head to tail.

"That fish smells delicious," Turtle said. "You are a good cook, Anansi. And you worked hard. I know, because I am very, very tired. Now it is time to eat the fish. When I eat by myself, I eat and get full. Since there are two of us, we should share the task. One of us should eat while the other gets full. Which do you want to do?"

"I want to get full!" Anansi said, thinking only of his stomach.

"Then I will eat." Turtle began to eat while Anansi lay back and waited for his stomach to get full.

"Are you full yet?" Turtle asked Anansi.
"Not yet. Keep eating."

Turtle ate some more. "Are you full yet?"
"No. Keep eating."

Turtle ate some more. "Are you full yet?"
"Not at all," Anansi said. "I'm as empty
as when you started."

"That's too bad," Turtle told him. "Because I'm full, and all the fish is gone."

"What?" Anansi cried. It was true. Turtle had eaten the whole fish. "You cheated me!" Anansi yelled when he realized what had happened.

"I did not!" Turtle replied.

"You did! You made me do all the work, then you ate the fish yourself. You won't get away with this. I am going to the Justice Tree."

Anansi ran to the Justice Tree. Warthog sat beneath its branches. Warthog was a fair and honest judge. All the animals brought their quarrels to him.

"What do you want, Anansi?" Warthog asked.

"I want justice," Anansi said. "Turtle cheated me. We went fishing together. He tricked me into doing all the work, then he ate the fish himself. Turtle deserves to be punished."

Warthog knew how lazy Anansi was. He couldn't imagine him working hard at anything. "Did you really do all the work?" he asked.

"Yes," Anansi replied.

"What did you do?"

"I wove the net.

I set it in the river.

I caught the fish,

and I cooked it."

"That is a lot of work. You must have gotten very tired."

"No," said Anansi. "I didn't get tired at all. Turtle got tired, not me."

Warthog frowned. "Turtle got tired? What did he do?"

"Nothing!"

"If he did nothing, why did he get tired? Anansi, I don't believe you. No one gets tired by doing nothing. If Turtle got tired, then he must have done all the work. You are not telling the truth. Go home now and stop making trouble."

Warthog had spoken. There was nothing more to be said. Anansi went home in disgrace, and it was a long time before he spoke to Turtle again.

But some good came out of it. Anansi learned how to weave nets and how to use them to catch food. He taught his friends how to do it, and they taught their friends. Soon spiders all over the world were weaving. To this day, wherever you find spiders, you will find their nets.

They are called "spider webs."

Think and Share

Talk About It What three rules would you give Anansi and Turtle to follow if they go fishing again?

1. The pictures below show what happens in the middle of the story. On another piece of paper draw what happens at the beginning and at the end of the story. **Retell**

2. What happens to make Anansi so angry? Look back at page 389. Read that part. **Cause and Effect**

3. A lot happens in this story. What did you do to make sure you didn't miss anything? **Monitor and Fix Up**

Look Back and Write Reread pages 390–393. Why didn't Justice Warthog believe Anansi's story? Use information from the story to support your answer.

Meet the Author
Eric Kimmel

Read more books by Eric Kimmel about Anansi.

Eric Kimmel first heard stories about Anansi as a child in New York City. He also heard Anansi stories from neighbors when he lived in the Virgin Islands. The stories come from Africa and are very old. "I enjoyed telling the stories so much that I tried my hand at writing them."

Mr. Kimmel says, "I like spiders. I never kill one. If I find a spider in the house, I catch it and take it outside. Spiders do us a lot of good, catching flies and other insect pests."

Meet the Illustrator
Janet Stevens

Before Janet Stevens drew Anansi, she read books about spiders. She thought about how to show Anansi's personality. "I mainly did it through his movement and gestures. He doesn't have a lot of face." She didn't want Anansi to look cute. "I like Anansi," she says. "He likes to get out of working."

Read two more books by Janet Stevens.

Ms. Stevens has written and illustrated many children's books. She enjoys drawing wrinkles. "My favorite characters are rhinos, iguanas—anything with lots of wrinkles."

Do spiders stick to their own webs?

by Amy Goldman Koss

The spider weaves a sticky web
To capture bugs to eat.
What keeps the spider's sticky web
From sticking to her feet?

Spiderwebs are very tricky
Because not all the strands are sticky.
Unlike the passing hapless fly,
The spider knows which strands are dry.

But if by accident she stands
On any of the sticky strands,
She still would not get stuck, you see—
Her oily body slides off free.

Write Now

Writing and Grammar

Advice

Prompt

In *Anansi Goes Fishing*, Warthog gives Anansi good advice. Think about a problem a friend might have. Now write advice to your friend.

Student Model

Writer tells what advice is about.

Most <u>sentences</u> are commands.

Here is how to catch the school bus on time. Set the alarm ten minutes earlier. Don't push the snooze button. Don't dawdle dressing and eating. Walk to the bus quickly. Leave at the same time every day. You won't ever miss the bus again.

Grammar

Verbs for Present, Past, and Future

Some verbs tell about now. They may end with **-s.** Some verbs tell about the past. They end with **-ed.** Some verbs tell about the future. They begin with **will.**

Today Anansi **waits** for Turtle.
Yesterday Anansi **waited** for Turtle.
Tomorrow Anansi **will wait** for Turtle.

Write these verbs from the advice sentences: *miss, push, dawdle, walk.* First make the verbs tell about the past. Then make the verbs tell about the future.

Let's Talk About
Creative Ideas

Words to Read

daughters
youngest
their
buy
many
alone
half

Read the Words

Rosa and Blanca are the daughters of a very loving mother. Rosa is the youngest. Their mother can't buy them many things, but she gives them lots of love. The two girls know that they will never be alone. They say that they will be happy if they can find in themselves half as much love as their mother gives.

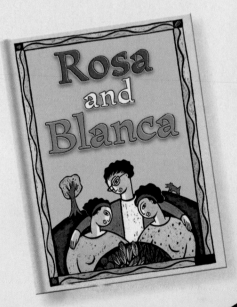

Genre: Realistic Fiction
Realistic fiction is a made-up story that could really happen. Next you will read about Rosa and Blanca, two sisters with a clever idea.

Rosa and Blanca

by Joe Hayes

illustrated by José Ortega

Who are Rosa and Blanca, and what is their creative idea?

Once there were two sisters named Rosa and Blanca. They loved each other very much. If their mother sent Rosa to the store to buy flour for tortillas, Blanca would go with her. If their mother told Blanca to sweep the sidewalk in front of their house, Rosa would help her.

Their mother would always say, "My daughters are so good to one another. They make me very happy. I think I am the luckiest mother in the town. No. I am the luckiest mother in the country. No. I am the luckiest mother in the whole world!"

When Rosa and Blanca grew up, Rosa got married. She and her husband had three children. Blanca didn't get married. She lived alone.

One year Rosa planted a garden. Blanca planted a garden too. They planted corn and tomatoes and good hot *chiles*.

When the tomatoes were round and ripe, Rosa helped Blanca pick the tomatoes in her garden. Blanca helped Rosa pick the tomatoes in her garden.

That night Rosa thought, "My poor sister Blanca lives all alone. She has no one to help her make a living. I have a husband and helpful children. I will give her half of my tomatoes to sell in the market."

Rosa filled a basket with tomatoes. She started toward Blanca's house.

That very same night Blanca thought, "My poor sister Rosa has a husband and three children. There are five to feed in her house. I only have myself. I will give her half of my tomatoes to sell in the market."

Blanca filled a basket with tomatoes. She started toward Rosa's house. The night was dark. The two sisters did not see each other when they passed.

Rosa added her tomatoes to the pile in Blanca's kitchen. Blanca added her tomatoes to the pile in Rosa's kitchen.

The next day, Rosa looked at her pile of tomatoes. "*¡Vaya!*" she said. "How can I have so many tomatoes? Did my tomatoes have babies during the night?"

The next day Blanca looked at her pile of tomatoes. "¡Vaya!" she said. "How can I have so many tomatoes? Did my tomatoes have babies during the night?"

When the corn was ripe, Rosa helped Blanca pick her corn. Blanca helped Rosa pick her corn.

That night Rosa thought, "I will give half of my corn to Blanca to sell in the market."

That night Blanca thought, "I will give half of my corn to Rosa to sell in the market."

Each sister filled a basket with corn. Rosa went to Blanca's house. Blanca went to Rosa's house. The night was dark. They did not see each other when they passed.

Rosa added her corn to the corn in Blanca's house. Blanca added her corn to the corn in Rosa's house.

The next day Rosa said, "¡Vaya! How can I have so much corn? Did each ear invite a friend to spend the night?"

The next day Blanca said, "¡Vaya! How can I have so much corn? Did each ear invite a friend to spend the night?"

When the chiles were red and hot, Rosa helped Blanca pick her chiles. Blanca helped Rosa pick her chiles.

That night Rosa thought, "I will give Blanca half of my chiles to sell in the market."

That night Blanca thought, "I will give Rosa half of my chiles to sell in the market."

Each sister filled a basket with chiles.

Just then Rosa's youngest child started to cry. Rosa went to the child's room. She picked him up and rocked him.

Blanca was on her way to Rosa's house.

When Rosa's child went to sleep, Rosa picked up her basket of chiles. She started out the door. Blanca was coming in the door.

They both said, "¡Vaya!"

Rosa said, "Blanca, what are you doing? Why do you have that basket of chiles?"

Blanca said, "Rosa, what are you doing? Why do you have that basket of chiles?"

Rosa said, "I was going to give half of my chiles to you."

Blanca said, "But I was going to give half of my chiles to you!" Both sisters laughed.

Rosa said, "So that is why I still had so many tomatoes!"

Blanca said, "So that is why I still had so much corn!" The sisters hugged each other.

The next day Rosa and Blanca went to their mother's house. They told their mother what they had done.

Their old mother smiled and hugged her daughters. She said, "My daughters are so good to one another. They make me very happy. I think I am the luckiest mother in the town. No. I am the luckiest mother in the country. No. I am the luckiest mother in the whole world!"

Think and Share

Talk About It Rosa and Blanca had a clever idea that went wrong. Now they are planting again. What will you tell them so that they will not have another mix-up?

1. Use the pictures below to retell the story. **Retell**

2. What was the big idea of this story? What do you think the characters learned? **Theme and Plot**

3. What did you predict the sisters would do with their vegetables? Were you right? Did you change any predictions as you read? **Predict**

Look Back and Write Look back in the story. Name three things that Rosa and Blanca planted.

About the Author
Joe Hayes

Joe Hayes grew up listening to stories told by his father. He liked hearing stories so much that he decided he wanted to tell them too. Mr. Hayes began by telling stories to his own children. He soon realized that he liked telling stories to as many children as he could!

Mr. Hayes travels to many different places to share with children the stories he has learned. He has also published 20 books, many in English and Spanish.

Read more books by Joe Hayes.

The Crow and the Pitcher

a fable by Aesop retold by Eric Blair
illustrated by Laura Ovresat

There was once a thirsty crow. She had flown a long way looking for water.

The thirsty crow saw a pitcher of water and flew down to drink.

The pitcher had only a little water left at the bottom.

The crow put her beak into the pitcher. The water was so low she couldn't reach it.

*But I must have water to drink.
I can't fly any farther,* thought
the crow.

I know. I'll tip the pitcher over,
she thought.

The thirsty crow beat the pitcher
with her wings, but she wasn't
strong enough to tip it.

*Maybe I can break the pitcher. Then
the water will flow,* thought the crow.

She backed away to get a
flying start. With all her might,
the thirsty crow flew at the
pitcher. She struck it with her
pointed beak and claws, but the
tired crow wasn't strong enough
to break the pitcher.

Just as she was about to give
up, the crow had another idea.
She dropped a pebble into the
pitcher. The water rose a little.

She dropped another and another. With each pebble, the water level rose more.

Soon the water reached the brim. The crow drank until she was no longer thirsty.

The crow was pleased with herself. By refusing to give up, she had solved her difficult problem.

Write Now

Writing and Grammar

Ad

Prompt

In *Rosa and Blanca*, two sisters grow vegetables.
Think about a new snack you could make with fruit or vegetables.
Now write an ad to tell people about your snack.

Student Model

Name of snack is in ad's title.

Vivid <u>word</u> <u>choice</u> makes new snack sound tasty.

Sentence attempts to persuade readers.

<u>Broc Puffs—A Tasty New Snack</u>
Ryan hated broccoli. Then a friend offered him Broc Puffs. Ryan loved the fresh taste. He loved the crispy crunch. Now he likes broccoli. Buy Broc Puffs today. You will love them too!

More About Verbs

Use the correct verb in a sentence to show that something is happening now, in the past, or in the future.

> Today they **plant** beans. (now)
> Yesterday they **planted** corn. (past)
> Tomorrow they **will plant** more. (future)

• •

Write the verbs in the ad. Write *N* if the verb tells about now, *P* if it tells about the past, and *F* if it tells about the future.

Let's Talk About
Creative Ideas

Words to Read

| neighbor |
| hours |
| money |
| clothes |
| taught |
| only |
| question |

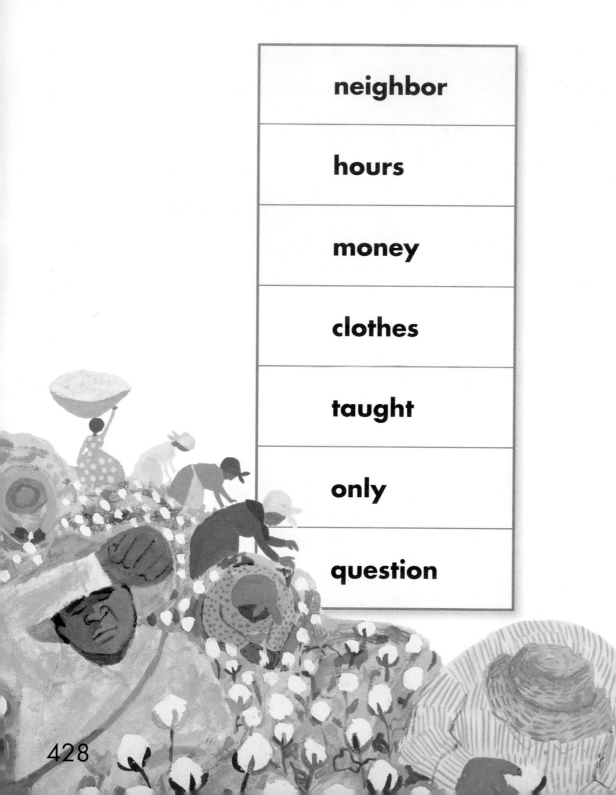

Read the Words

   Our neighbor spends many hours in his beautiful garden. He doesn't make a lot of money, and he wears torn clothes. However, he loves his plants and flowers. He taught himself a lot of what he knows. I have only one question for him. Can he teach me too?

A Weed Is a Flower

Genre: Biography
A biography tells about a real person's life. It is written by another person. Next you will read the biography of George Washington Carver, a creative scientist.

A Weed Is a Flower

The Life of George Washington Carver

by Aliki

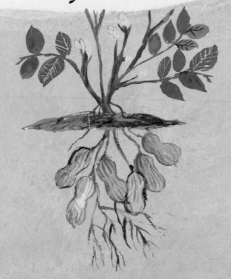

Who was George Washington Carver?

George Washington Carver was born in Missouri in 1860—more than a hundred years ago. It was a terrible time. Mean men rode silently in the night, kidnapping slaves from their owners and harming those who tried to stop them.

One night, a band of these men rode up to the farm of Moses Carver, who owned George and his mother, Mary. Everyone ran in fear. But before Mary could hide her baby, the men came and snatched them both, and rode away into the night.

Moses Carver sent a man to look for them. Mary was never found. But in a few days, the man returned with a small bundle wrapped in his coat and tied to the back of his saddle. It was the baby, George.

Moses and his wife, Susan, cared for Mary's children. George remained small and weak. But as he grew, they saw he was an unusual child. He wanted to know about everything around him. He asked about the rain, the flowers, and the insects. He asked questions the Carvers couldn't answer.

When he was very young, George kept a garden where he spent hours each day caring for his plants. If they weren't growing well, he found out why. Soon they were healthy and blooming. In winter he covered his plants to protect them. In spring he planted new seeds. George looked after each plant as though it was the only one in his garden.

Neighbors began to ask George's advice about their plants, and soon he was known as the Plant Doctor.

As time went on, George wondered about more and more things. He wanted to learn and yearned to go to school.

In the meantime, the slaves had been freed, but schools nearby were not open to blacks. So when he was ten, George left his brother, his garden, and the Carver farm and went off to find the answers to his questions.

Wherever George Washington Carver found schools, he stayed. He worked for people to earn his keep. He scrubbed their floors, washed their clothes, and baked their bread. Whatever George did, he did well. Even the smallest chore was important to him.

Some people took George in as their son. First he stayed with Mariah and Andy Watkins, who were like parents to him. Then he moved to Kansas and lived with "Aunt" Lucy and "Uncle" Seymour. They, too, loved this quiet boy who was so willing to help.

George worked hard for many years, always trying to save enough money for college. Other boys, who had parents to help them, were able to enter college much sooner than George. He was thirty before he had saved enough. Still, it was not that simple. Not all colleges would admit blacks, even if they had the money to pay.

George was not discouraged. He moved to Iowa and found a college which was glad to have a black student.

At college, George continued to work. He opened a laundry where he washed his schoolmates' clothes.

And, he continued to learn. His teachers and friends soon realized that this earnest young man was bursting with talents. He played the piano, he sang beautifully, and he was an outstanding painter. In fact, for a time he thought of becoming an artist.

439

But the more George thought of what he wanted to do, the more he wanted to help his people. And he remembered that his neighbors used to call him the Plant Doctor.

He had never forgotten his love for plants. In all the years he had wandered, he always had something growing in his room.

So, George Washington Carver chose to study agriculture. He learned about plants, flowers, and soil. He learned the names of the weeds. Even they were important to him. He often said: a weed is a flower growing in the wrong place.

He still asked questions. If no person or book could answer them, he found the answers himself. He experimented with his own plants, and found secrets no one else knew.

When George finished college, he began to teach. He was asked to go to Alabama, where a college for blacks needed his talent. It was there, at Tuskegee Institute, that George Washington Carver made his life.

In Alabama, Professor Carver taught his students and the poor black farmers, who earned their livelihood from the soil. He taught them how to make their crops grow better.

443

Most of the farmers raised cotton. But sometimes the crops were destroyed by rain or insects, and the farmers couldn't earn enough to eat.

Professor Carver told them to plant other things as well. Sweet potatoes and peanuts were good crops. They were easy to grow. He said that raising only cotton harmed the soil. It was better if different crops were planted each year.

The farmers did not want to listen. They were afraid to plant peanuts and sweet potatoes. They were sure that no one would buy them.

But Professor Carver had experimented in his laboratory. He had found that many things could be made from the sweet potato. He made soap, coffee, and starch. He made more than a hundred things from the sweet potato.

And even though people in those days called peanuts "monkey food," Professor Carver said they were good for people, too. Besides, he found that still more things could be made from the peanut. Paper, ink, shaving cream, sauces, linoleum, shampoo, and even milk! In fact, he made three hundred different products from the peanut.

Once, when important guests were expected at Tuskegee, Dr. Carver chose the menu. The guests sat around the table and enjoyed a meal of soup, creamed mock chicken, bread, salad, coffee, candy, cake, and ice cream. Imagine their surprise when they learned that the meal was made entirely from peanuts!

Slowly, the farmers listened to George Washington Carver. They planted peanuts and sweet potatoes. Before they knew it these became two of the most important crops in Alabama.

Soon the whole country knew about Dr. Carver and the great things he was doing. He was honored by Presidents and other important people. Every day, his mailbox bulged with letters from farmers and scientists who wanted his advice. He was offered great sums of money, which he turned down. Money was not important to him. He did not even bother to cash many of the checks he received.

Throughout his life, George Washington Carver asked nothing of others. He sought only to help. He lived alone and tended to his own needs. He washed his clothes and patched them, too. He used the soap he made and ate the food he grew.

Dr. Carver was asked to speak in many parts of the world, but he did not leave Tuskegee often. He had things to do. He continued to paint. He worked in his greenhouse and in his laboratory, where he discovered many things. He discovered that dyes could be made from plants, and colors from the Alabama clay. Even when he was over eighty and close to death, Dr. Carver kept working. Night after night, while the rest of the town lay asleep, a light still shone in his window.

The baby born with no hope for the future grew into one of the great scientists of his country. George Washington Carver, with his goodness and devotion, helped not only his own people, but all peoples of the world.

Think and Share

Talk About It If you could visit Dr. Carver, would you visit when he was a boy, a young man, or a famous professor? Tell about your visit.

1. Use the pictures below to summarize what you learned. **Retell**

2. Why did the farmers start planting peanuts and sweet potatoes? **Cause and Effect**

3. How did you look for the answer to question 2? Did you read every word? Did you skim and scan? Which way is best? Why? **Monitor and Fix Up**

Look Back and Write Look back at page 445. Why did Dr. Carver tell farmers to plant sweet potatoes and peanuts?

About the Author and Illustrator
Aliki

When Aliki writes a book, she often uses cartoons and draws funny characters talking in the margins. Her books are fun, but she does lots of research. "I spend many hours at my desk," she says. "Some books take three years to finish. That's why I call what I do hard fun."

Aliki grew up in Philadelphia, but her parents are from Greece. She speaks Greek as well as English. She prefers to use only her first name on her books.

Read two more books by Aliki.

What's Made from Corn?

If you are writing a report, you can use the Internet to help find information. Maria wants to give a report on how corn is used every day. She does an Internet search using a search engine. First, Maria brainstorms a list of keywords about her topic. These can be single words or groups of words that she will type into the search window of a search engine. Maria came up with these keywords:

Corn

Uses of corn

How we use corn

She can type any of these into a search engine window and then click the Search button. After a few seconds, she gets a list of Web sites.

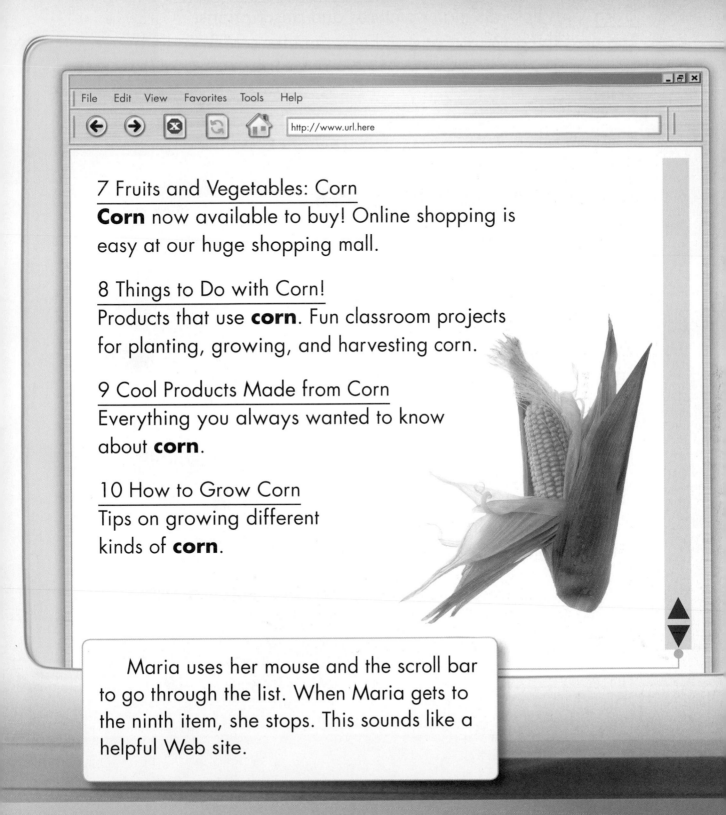

7 Fruits and Vegetables: Corn
Corn now available to buy! Online shopping is easy at our huge shopping mall.

8 Things to Do with Corn!
Products that use **corn**. Fun classroom projects for planting, growing, and harvesting corn.

9 Cool Products Made from Corn
Everything you always wanted to know about **corn**.

10 How to Grow Corn
Tips on growing different kinds of **corn**.

Maria uses her mouse and the scroll bar to go through the list. When Maria gets to the ninth item, she stops. This sounds like a helpful Web site.

Maria clicks on the link <u>Cool Products Made from Corn</u>. This link has many pictures and descriptions. The next thing Maria sees on her computer screen is:

Cool Products Made from Corn

- Corn can be used to make knives, forks, and spoons. Corn can be used to make plates, diapers, milk jugs, razors, and golf tees. All these things dissolve when put into the garbage. This helps the environment.

- Corn can be made into "packing peanuts." Packing peanuts are used to protect objects packed in boxes. These peanuts dissolve in water.

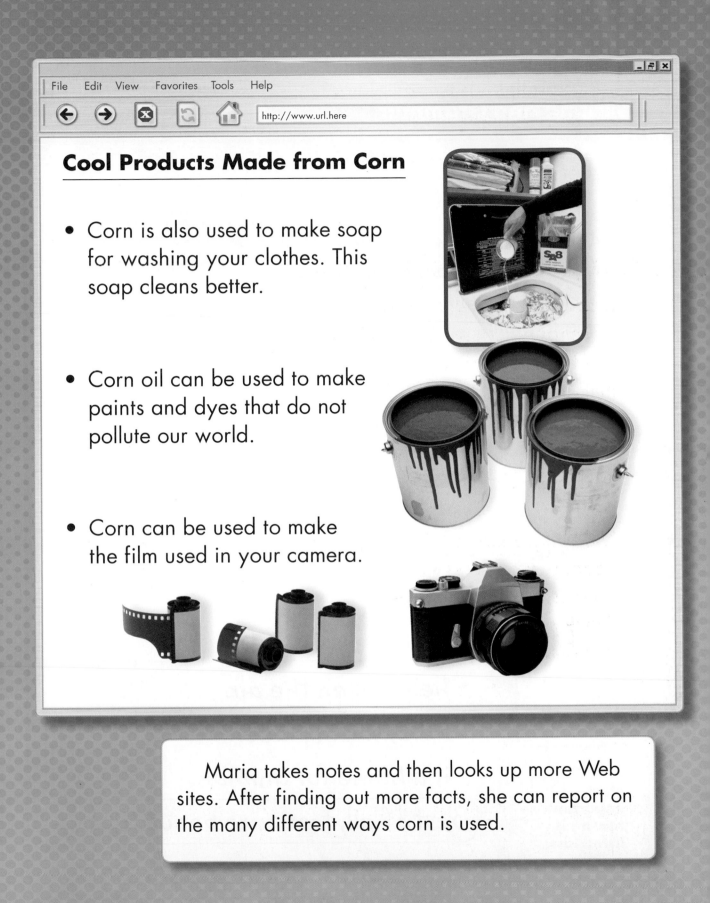

Cool Products Made from Corn

- Corn is also used to make soap for washing your clothes. This soap cleans better.

- Corn oil can be used to make paints and dyes that do not pollute our world.

- Corn can be used to make the film used in your camera.

Maria takes notes and then looks up more Web sites. After finding out more facts, she can report on the many different ways corn is used.

Write Now

Writing and Grammar

Poster

Prompt

In *A Weed Is a Flower,* a scientist convinces farmers to plant peanuts. Think about something you want people to plant.

Now write a poster that tells what they should plant and why.

Student Model

Title tells what poster is about.

Writer <u>focuses</u> on one <u>idea</u> throughout poster.

Most important reason is listed last.

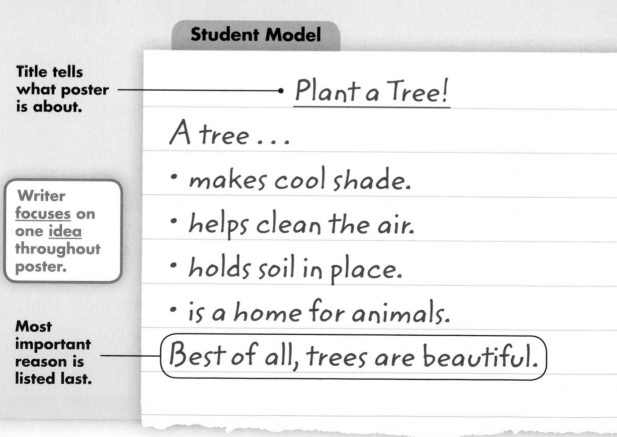

Plant a Tree!

A tree . . .

• makes cool shade.

• helps clean the air.

• holds soil in place.

• is a home for animals.

Best of all, trees are beautiful.

458

Grammar

Am, Is, Are, Was, and Were

The verbs **am, is, are, was,** and **were** show what someone or something is or was. They are forms of the verb *to be.*

Am, is, and **are** tell about now. **Was** and **were** tell about the past.

Use **am, is,** and **was** to tell about one person, place, or thing. Use **are** and **were** to tell about more than one.

• •

Look at the poster. Write the verbs that are forms of the verb *to be.*

Write a Letter

Juno and his grandma sent letters to each other. Choose a character from one of the stories in this unit. Write a letter to him or her. What would you write? Will you give Wagner advice? Will you tell Anansi a joke? Be creative. Use words in your letter, but also include a picture or other object that will mean something to your character.

Dear Anansi,

What does it mean to be creative?

Creative Characters

connect to
SOCIAL
STUDIES

Each story you read in this unit had at least one character who was creative. With a group, talk about each story. Tell how the characters acted in creative ways. Tell how an idea from each story could help you do something in a creative way. Make a chart of your ideas.

Story	Character	What they did	My idea

Step by Step

connect to
SCIENCE

When Pearl made a robot for her science project, she explained what she was doing step by step. Think of a creative project you might do. Write a set of step-by-step directions that someone else could follow.

How to make a chocolate chip pizza

What you need:
pizza dough
chocolate chips
strawberries
whipped cream

What you do:
First you spread the dough on the pan.

461

agriculture • buried

Aa

agriculture (ag ruh KUL cher) **Agriculture** is farming and growing crops. *NOUN*

amazing (uh MAY zing) Something that is **amazing** is very surprising: The hero made an **amazing** escape. *ADJECTIVE*

astronaut

astronaut (ASS truh nawt) An **astronaut** is a person who has been trained to fly in a spacecraft. While in space, **astronauts** repair space stations and do experiments. *NOUN*

Bb

brave (BRAYV) If you are **brave**, you are not afraid: The **brave** girl pulled her little brother away from the burning leaves. *ADJECTIVE*

buried (BAIR eed) If you have **buried** something, you have hidden or covered it up: It was so cold that she **buried** her head under the covers. *VERB*

Cc

cactus

cactus (KAK tuhss) A **cactus** is a plant with sharp parts but no leaves. Most **cactuses** grow in very hot, dry areas of North and South America. Many have bright flowers. *NOUN*

challenge (CHAL lunj) To **challenge** is to call or invite someone to a game or contest: The knight **challenged** his rival to fight a duel. *VERB*

chiles (CHIL ayz) **Chiles** are a green or red pepper with a hot taste. *NOUN*

climate (KLY mit) **Climate** is the kind of weather a place has. *NOUN*

clutched (KLUCHT) To **clutch** is to hold something tightly: I **clutched** the railing to keep from falling. *VERB*

collar (KOL er) A **collar** is a band that is put around the neck of a dog or other pet. **Collars** can be made of leather or plastic. *NOUN*

college (KOL ij) **College** is the school that you go to after high school: After I finish high school, I plan to go to **college** to become a teacher. *NOUN*

coyote

coyote (ky OH tee or KY oht) A **coyote** is a small animal that looks something like a wolf. **Coyotes** have light yellow fur and bushy tails. *NOUN*

dam (DAM) A **dam** is a wall built to hold back the water of a creek, lake, or river. *NOUN*

dangerous (DAYN jer uhss) Something that is **dangerous** is not safe: Skating on thin ice is **dangerous**. *ADJECTIVE*

delicious (di LISH uhss) When something is **delicious**, it tastes or smells very good: The cookies were **delicious**. *ADJECTIVE*

desert (DEZ ert) A **desert** is a place without water or trees but with a lot of sand. It is usually hot. *NOUN*

desert

drooled (DROOLD) To **drool** is to let saliva run from the mouth like a baby sometimes does. The dog **drooled** when it saw the bone. *VERB*

Ee

electricity (i lek TRISS uh tee) **Electricity** is a kind of energy that makes light and heat. **Electricity** also runs motors. **Electricity** makes light bulbs shine, radios and televisions play, and cars start. *NOUN*

embarrassed (em BAIR uhst) When you feel **embarrassed**, you feel that people are thinking of you badly because of something you said or did: When I realized that I had given the wrong answer, I was **embarrassed**. *ADJECTIVE*

envelope (EN vuh lohp) An **envelope** is a folded paper cover. An **envelope** is used to mail a letter or something else that is flat. *NOUN*

excitement (ek SYT muhnt) **Excitement** happens when you have very strong, happy feelings about something that you like. *NOUN*

experiment (ek SPAIR uh muhnt) An **experiment** is a test to find out something: We do **experiments** in science class. *NOUN*

experiment

Gg

gnaws (NAWS) When an animal **gnaws**, it is biting and wearing away by biting: The brown mouse **gnaws** the cheese. *VERB*

gravity (GRAV uh tee) **Gravity** is the natural force that causes objects to move toward the center of the Earth. **Gravity** causes objects to have weight. *NOUN*

greenhouse (GREEN howss) A **greenhouse** is a building with a glass or plastic roof and sides. A **greenhouse** is kept warm and full of light for growing plants. *NOUN*

greenhouse

Hh

halfway (HAF WAY) To be **halfway** is to be in the middle: He was **halfway** through running the race. *ADVERB*

harsh (HARSH) To be **harsh** is to be rough, unpleasant, and unfriendly: The **harsh** weather made us stay indoors. *ADJECTIVE*

467

hooves (HUVZ or HOOVZ) **Hooves** are the hard part of the feet of some animals. Horses, cattle, sheep, moose, deer, and pigs have hooves. *NOUN*

Jj

justice (JUHS tis) **Justice** happens when things are right and fair. *NOUN*

Ll

laboratory (LAB ruh tor ee) A **laboratory** is a room where scientists work and do experiments and tests. *NOUN*

ladder

ladder (LAD er) A **ladder** is a set of steps between two long pieces of wood, metal, or rope. **Ladders** are used for climbing up and down. *NOUN*

lantern

lanterns (LAN ternz) **Lanterns** are portable lamps with coverings around them to protect them from wind and rain. *NOUN*

lazy (LAY zee) If a person is **lazy**, he or she does not want to work hard or to move fast: The **lazy** cat lay on the rug all day. *ADJECTIVE*

lodge (LOJ) A **lodge** is a den of an animal: The beavers built a **lodge**. *NOUN*

luckiest (LUHK ee est) The **luckiest** person is the one who has had the best fortune. *ADJECTIVE*

lumbered (LUHM berd) To **lumber** is to move along heavily and noisily: The old truck **lumbered** down the road. *VERB*

Mm

meadow (MED oh) A **meadow** is a piece of land where grass grows: There are sheep in the **meadow**. *NOUN*

meadow

mill (MIL) A **mill** is a building in which grain is ground into flour or meal. *NOUN*

monsters (MON sterz) **Monsters** are make-believe people or animals that are scary. In stories, some **monsters** are friendly, and others are not: Dragons are **monsters**. *NOUN*

musician (myoo ZISH uhn) A **musician** is a person who sings, plays, or writes music. *NOUN*

Nn

narrator (NAIR ayt or) A **narrator** is a person who tells a story or play. In a play, a **narrator** keeps the action moving. *NOUN*

Pp

persimmons (puhr SIM uhns) **Persimmons** are round, yellow and orange fruits about the size of plums. *NOUN*

persimmons

photograph (FOH tuh graf) A **photograph** is a picture you make with a camera. *NOUN*

Rr

relatives (REL uh tivs) Your **relatives** are the people who belong to the same family as you do: Your mother, sister, and cousin are all your **relatives**. *NOUN*

riverbank (RIV er bangk) A **riverbank** is the land on the side of a river or stream. *NOUN*

robbers (ROB ers) **Robbers** are people who rob or steal: The police chased the bank **robbers**. *NOUN*

robot (ROH bot or ROH BUHT) A **robot** is a machine that is run by a computer. **Robots** help people do work. **Robots** can look like people. *NOUN*

roller skate (ROH ler SKAYT) To **roller-skate** is to move by using **roller skates**, which are shoes that have wheels. *VERB/NOUN*

roller skates

Ss

shivered (SHIV erd) To **shiver** is to shake with cold, fear, or excitement: I **shivered** in the cold wind. *VERB*

shuttle (SHUHT uhl) A **shuttle** is a spacecraft with wings, which can orbit the earth, land like an airplane, and be used again. *NOUN*

471

slipped (SLIPT) When you **slip** you slide suddenly and unexpectedly: She **slipped** on the ice. *VERB*

smudged (SMUDJD) If something is **smudged**, it is marked with a dirty streak. *ADJECTIVE*

snuggled

snuggled (SNUHG uhld) To **snuggle** is to lie closely and comfortably together; cuddle: The kittens **snuggled** together in the basket. *VERB*

spirit (SPIR it) To have **spirit** is to have enthusiasm, courage, and loyalty: My sister has team **spirit**. *NOUN*

Tt

telescope (TEL uh skohp) A **telescope** is something you look through to make things far away seem nearer and larger: We looked at the moon through a **telescope**. *NOUN*

terrific (tuh RIF ik) To be **terrific** means to be very good, wonderful. She is a **terrific** tennis player. *ADJECTIVE*

Thanksgiving (thangks GIV ing) **Thanksgiving** is a holiday in November. *NOUN*

tortillas (tor TEE uhs) **Tortillas** are thin, flat, round breads usually made of cornmeal. *NOUN*

trash (TRASH) **Trash** is anything of no use or that is worn out. **Trash** is garbage or things to be thrown away. *NOUN*

trash

Ww

wad (WOD) A **wad** is a small, soft ball or chunk of something: She stepped in a **wad** of chewing gum. *NOUN*

weave (WEEV) To **weave** is to form threads into cloth. *VERB*

Tested Words

Unit 1
Iris and Walter

someone
somewhere
friend
country
beautiful
front

Exploring Space with an Astronaut

everywhere
live
work
woman
machines
move
world

Henry and Mudge and the Starry Night

couldn't
love
build
mother
bear
father
straight

A Walk in the Desert

water
eyes
early
animals
full
warm

The Strongest One

together
very
learn
often
though
gone
pieces

Unit 2

Tara and Tiree, Fearless Friends

family
once
pull
listen
heard
break

Ronald Morgan Goes to Bat

laugh
great
you're
either
certainly
second
worst

Turtle's Race with Beaver

enough
toward
above
ago
word
whole

The Bremen Town Musicians

people
sign
shall
bought
probably
pleasant
scared

A Turkey for Thanksgiving

door
behind
brought
minute
promise
sorry
everybody

Unit 3
Pearl and Wagner

science
shoe
won
guess
village
pretty
watch

Dear Juno

picture
school
answer
wash
parents
company
faraway

Anansi Goes Fishing

today
whatever
caught
believe
been
finally
tomorrow

Rosa and Blanca

their
many
alone
buy
half
youngest
daughters

A Weed Is a Flower

only
question
clothes
money
hours
neighbor
taught

Acknowledgments

Illustrations

Cover: Scott Gustafson; **158-159, 244-245, 275, 312-313, 339, 397, 420-423, 453, 460-461** Laura Ovresat; **129-150, 160** Courtesy David Diaz; **153** Derek Grinnell; **163-181** Scott Gustafson; **246** Russell Farrell; **253-273** Jon Goodell; **314** Bill Mayer; **344-345** Gideon Kendall

Photographs

Every effort has been made to secure permission and provide appropriate credit for photographic material. The publisher deeply regrets any omission and pledges to correct errors called to its attention in subsequent editions.

Unless otherwise acknowledged, all photographs are the property of Scott Foresman, a division of Pearson Education.

Photo locators denoted as follows: Top (T), Center (C), Bottom (B), Left (L), Right (R), Background (Bkgd).

10 (Bkgd) ©A. Witte/C. Mahaney/Getty Images, (C) Digital Vision; **12** (Bkgd) ©Doug Armand/Getty Images, (CR) ©Phil Schermeister/Corbis; **13** (TR, CL) ©Ariel Skelley/Corbis; **42** (Bkgd) ©Shilo Sports/Getty Images, (BC) ©Royalty-Free/Corbis; **43** (TR) ©George Hall/Corbis, (CL) ©Museum of Flight/Corbis, (BR) ©NASA; **44** Corbis; **45** (TR, CR) ©NASA, (BR) ©Royalty-Free/Corbis, (Bkgd) Getty Images; **46** (Bkgd, T, C, B) Getty Images; **47-51** ©NASA; **52** (B) ©NASA/Roger Ressmeyer/Corbis; **53-58** ©NASA; **60** Getty Images; **62** (CC) Getty Images, (Bkdg) ©Royalty-Free/Corbis; **63** (T) Corbis, (CR, C) ©Richard T. Nowitz/Corbis, (BR) ©Joseph Sohm/ChromoSohm Inc./Corbis; **64** (B, TR) ©Richard T. Nowitz/Corbis; **65** (TR) ©Franz-Marc Frei/Corbis, (BR) ©Richard T. Nowitz/Corbis; **66** NASA; **67** ©NASA; **68** (Bkgd) ©Jim Ballard/Getty Images, (CL) ©Joe McDonald/Corbis, (BR) Digital Vision; **69** (CL) ©Nigel J. Dennis/Gallo Images/Corbis, (TR) ©Michael & Patricia Fogden/Corbis; **90** ©Gabe Palmer/Corbis; **92** (BL) Getty Images, (T, BR) ©Roger Ressmeyer/Corbis; **93** (T)© Roger Ressmeyer/Corbis, (BL) ©Bill and Sally Fletcher; **96** (Bkgd) ©George H. H. Huey/Corbis, (CL) ©Altrendo Nature/Getty Images, (BR) ©Galen Rowell/Corbis; **97** (TL) Digital Vision, (CR) Brand X Pictures, (BR) ©Steve Maslowski/Visuals Unlimited; **98** (BC) ©David A. Northcott/Corbis, (TL) ©Ralph Hopkins/Lonely Planet Images; **99** (TR) ©Tim Flach/Stone, (Bkgd) Getty Images, (BR) ©David Muench/Corbis; **100** Getty Images; **101** ©Maryellen Baker/Botanica; **102** (BL) ©Jeri Gleiter/Getty Images, (Bkgd) Getty Images, (BR) ©Marco Simoni/Robert Harding Picture Library Ltd.; **103** (CL) ©Ron Thomas/Getty Images, (B) ©Robert Van Der Hilst/Getty Images; **104** ©Paul McCormick/Getty Images; **105** (BR) ©Bates Littlehales/NGS Image Collection, (BL) ©David Muench/Corbis, (CR) ©Gary W. Carter/Corbis; **106** (CR) ©Charles C. Place/Getty Images, (TC) ©Ralph Hopkins/Lonely Planet Images, (Bkgd) Getty Images; **107** (C) ©David Maitland/Getty Images, (TR) ©David Aubrey/Getty Images, (TC, C) ©Jack Dykinga/Getty Images; **108** (BC) Getty Images, (Bkgd) ©Arthur S. Aubry/Getty Images, (C) ©Steve Maslowski/Visuals Unlimited; **109** (TR) ©George D. Lepp/Corbis, (BR) ©David A. Northcott/Corbis, (CL) ©Joe McDonald/Corbis; **110** (BL) ©Farrell Grehan/Corbis, (Bkgd) Digital Vision, (BR) ©Shai Ginott/Corbis; **111** ©Tom Bean/Corbis; **112** ©Joe McDonald/Corbis; **113** (BR) Getty Images, (BL) ©Jonathan Blair/NGS Image Collection, (CR) ©David Muench/Corbis; **114** (Bkgd, BL) Getty Images, (BR) ©Michael & Patricia Fogden/Corbis; **115** (TR) ©Mel Yates/Getty Images, (BR, TL) Getty Images; **116** (BL) ©Tom Bean/Getty Images, (Bkgd) ©Arthur Tilley/Getty Images, (BR) ©Layne Kennedy/Corbis; **117** ©Matthias Clamer/Getty Images; **118** (CL) ©Tim Flach/Stone, (CR) ©William J. Hebert/Getty Images, (Bkgd) ©Ira Rubin/Getty Images; **119** (BC) ©Ira Rubin/Getty Images, (TL) ©Royalty-Free/Corbis, (CR) ©Jean Paul Ferrero/Ardea, (TR) ©Rogier Gruys; **120** ©Steve Maslowski/Visuals Unlimited; **124** (CL) ©Gary Braasch/Corbis, (BL) ©Theo Allofs/Corbis; **125** (CL) ©Tom Brakefield/Corbis, (TL) ©Bill Varie/Corbis; **127** ©Robert Van Der Hilst/Getty Images; **129** (TL) ©Ron Watts/Corbis, (TR) ©Martin Harvey/Peter Arnold, Inc.; **152** ©Tom Brakefield/Corbis; **153** ©Tom Brakefield/Corbis; **154** (T) ©Roland Seitre/Peter Arnold, Inc., (B) ©John H. Hoffman/Bruce Coleman Inc.; **155** ©Theo Allofs/Corbis; **158** (BL) ©A. Witte/C. Mahaney/Getty Images, (BC) Digital Vision; **159** Getty Images; **162** ©Brand X Pictures/Getty Images; **163** (TL) ©Matthew Polak/Corbis, (CR) ©AFP/Getty Images, (BL) Getty Images; **183** (TL) Photo of Andrew Clements used with permission of Simon & Schuster, Inc. ©Bill Crofton, (CL) Brand X Pictures; **184** ©Tim Davis/Corbis; **185** (TL) ©Andrea Comas/Corbis, (CL) ©Jean-Bernard Vernier/Corbis, (BL) ©Tom Nebbia/Corbis; **186** (Bkgd) ©Owen Franken/Corbis, (TR) ©Vaughn Youtz/Corbis, (CR) ©Armando Arorizo/Corbis, (CL) ©Shamil Zhumatov/Corbis; **187** (TL) ©Kai Pfaffenbach/Corbis, (BR) ©Ralf-Finn Hestoft/Corbis; **190** (Bkgd) ©Royalty-Free/Corbis, (CL) ©Brand X Pictures/Getty Images, (BR) ©Julia Fishkin/Getty Images; **191** (CL) ©CLEO Freelance/Index Stock Imagery, (TR) BananaStock; **218** ©Kennan Ward/Corbis; **219** ©Royalty-Free/Corbis; **247** Getty Images; **252** ©Ariel Skelley/Corbis; **253** (CR) ©Michael Pole/Corbis, (TR) ©Paul Harris/Getty Images; **276** (Bkgd) ©Dex Image/Getty Images, (B) ©Darryl Torckler/Getty Images; **277** Getty Images; **278** (T) ©Ariadne Van Zandbergen/Lonely Planet Images, (TR) ©Eric and David Hosking/Corbis, (CL) ©Lester Lefkowitz/Getty Images, (CL) ©Cliff Beittel, (B) ©Peter Cade/Getty Images; **279** (B) ©Winifred Wisniewski/Frank Lane Picture Agency/Corbis, (CL) ©Nigel J. Dennis/Gallo Images/Corbis, (T) ©Ian Beames/Ardea; **282** (CL) ©Tom Stewart/Corbis, (BR) ©Ariel Skelley/Corbis, (Bkgd) ©Digital Vision/Getty Images; **283** (TL) ©Ariel Skelley/Corbis, (CL) ©Steve Satushek/Getty Images, (TR) ©Brooklyn Productions/Getty Images; **304** Getty Images; **305** (BR) ©Royalty-Free/Corbis, (T) Brand X Pictures; **307** (CR) ©Catherine Karnow/Corbis, (CL) ©Kevin Fleming/Corbis; **308** (BR) ©Jose Luis Pelaez, Inc/Corbis, (TR) Corbis; **309** ©Larry Williams/Corbis; **312** Getty Images; **316** (Bkgd) ©Comstock, Inc., (C) ©Jim Cummins/Getty Images; **317** (T) ©Jose Luis Pelaez, Inc/Corbis, (BL) ©Mike Timo/Getty Images; **340** (BL) ©Roger Ressmeyer/